Guard Duty

Intercession from a Military Perspective

Catherine F. Tukes & Kena P. Jones

Guard Duty
Copyright © 2016 by Catherine F. Tukes & Kena P. Jones
All rights reserved. No part of this publication may be reproduced, stored in or introduced into a retrieval system, or transmitted in any form or by any means (electronic, mechanical, photocopying, recording or otherwise) except for brief quotations in printed reviews, without he prior written permission of the publisher or author(s) of this book. Scripture taken from the Holy Bible, King James Version, Crown Copyright in UK, The Holy Bible, New Century Version, Copyright © 2005 Thomas Nelson. Bible Concordance Copyright © 1991, 2000 by AMG Publishers. Used by permission. All rights reserved.
ISBN: 0990386929
ISBN: 9780990386926
Printed in the United States of America
Cover Design
Copyright © 2016
By CatLaw Creative Solutions
Photos: Fire ID 264885
Tower images4K8Y8BHP9
Eyes imagesUKYA0OA

This book is dedicated to all prayer warriors, intercessors, and children of the Most High God, true soldiers on the battle field…

ACKNOWLEDGMENTS

I would like to acknowledge the King of Kings, Lord of Lords, and my Savior Jesus Christ for endowing me with the gift of writing. I am grateful for my husband, Lawan, my four wonderful children: Jared, Ty'Lar, Aryanna, and Tiara. To my mother, Virginia Febo, and to my best friend and co-worker in the Gospel, Kena Jones who has always supported me as a writer and said "Yes" when I invited her to come on this journey with me. I also would like to thank my Pastor, J. Calvin Tibbs who has written such a wonderful foreword and has been an amazing teacher to me and my children. Thanks to Dr. Robert Gaines my friend and former Pastor for the words of encouragement. Thank you to a host of friends who have been faithfully buying and supporting all of my writing endeavors. Thanks Mother Alice Smith for giving me the idea and concept for the book cover of this book.

Many Blessings,
Catherine Tukes

First and foremost I thank God for being who HE is in my life, for HIS amazing love and for the gifts and talents he has given me. I would like to also thank my wonderful husband, Hawathar Jones, and my two beautiful children, Akeyla and A 'Jay Jones. I would also like to give special thanks to my mother Patricia who is my inspiration. I am so grateful for my best friend and sister in Christ, Catherine Tukes for her encouragement for me to write. She's always there pushing me to write.

In Christ,
Kena Jones

FOREWORD

Catherine F. Tukes and Kena P. Jones have put together a stellar approach to winning in warfare. As every Army soldier and former military personnel knows, "Guard Duty" is a part of the job – it's everyone's responsibility. And so it is in our service to God – everyone has "Guard Duty!"

Tukes and Jones lay out the plan for our involvement in battles that are invisible, fire fights that appear out of nowhere, and what to do instructions when things get "set off." You will be glad to know that you have orders, procedures and weapons with which to defend your post!

Inside these pages you will discover the power principles of the prayer lives of great men. From the prophet Ezekiel to the apostle Paul, "Guard Duty" will challenge you to step into your role as a warrior for God. Men and women alike will benefit from the principals contained within this book. For some, they will be upgraded to stellar levels of effectiveness. For others, they will gain strength from the ground floor – up. At every level, God's Kingdom here on earth will expand because of the fire power made available through the fervent efforts of those who serve Him, while on "Guard Duty".

J. Calvin Tibbs
Pastor
Kingdom Dominion Church
Villa Rica, Ga

CATHERINE F. TUKES & KENA P. JONES

We have been given a rich legacy of the power and importance of prayer, both in scripture and throughout Christian history. Every generation needs courageous believers who will trust God at HIS Word and pick up the baton of intercession, continuing the powerful legacy of faithfully standing in the gap and seeking HIS heart in prayer.

This book will enrich your relationship with the Lord and equip you to walk closer to HIM becoming a more committed soldier for the LORD and effective prayer warrior for HIS glory.

I highly recommend this book the authors are living examples of its contents!

Dr. Robert L. Gaines
Pastor, Greater New Birth Jerusalem Ministries, Inc.
Clarksville, TN

TABLE OF CONTENTS

Acknowledgments — v
Foreword — vii
Introduction — xi
The Watchman Creed — xiii
Sound the Alarm! — xv

Part One — 1
1 Terminology — 3
2 Guard Composition — 7
3 General Orders — 10
4 Guard Shifts/Prayer Watches — 15

Part Two Prayer Modules — 21
5 Prayer vs. Intercession — 23
6 The Lord's Prayer (Jesus's Prayer Module) — 29
7 The Weapons of our Warfare (Paul's Prayer Module) — 38
8 Daniel's Prayer Module — 44
9 Paul's Prayer Module (Part 2) — 48
10 Exploring Ezekiel's Prayer Module — 55
11 Hosea's Prayer Life — 60

Part Three Short and Simple Prayer Starters   63

Part Four   75
12 Reports on the Enemy   77
13 Identifying the Threat Level   83
14 Disabling the Strong Man   89

About the Author   95
Reference Page   97

INTRODUCTION

"I have set watchmen upon thy walls O' Jerusalem which shall never hold their peace day or night ye that make mention of the Lord, keep not silence."

Isaiah 62:6 (KJV)

"Jerusalem, I have put GUARDS on the walls to watch. They must not be silent day or night. You People who remind the Lord of your needs in prayer should never be quiet."

(NCV)

Purpose and Scope
This manual is for intercessors, and prayer warriors concerned with the organization and functions of the interior and exterior guards. It includes biblical references and examples of prayer modules right from the Word of God. It also covers orders, the main duties and responsibilities of a "watchman" or a "guard." Some of the structure is adapted from the Army Field Manual 22-6 and converted into Christian principles under the sole leadership and inspiration of the Holy Spirit.

As the manual is a guide, and as all possible situations and eventualities cannot be foreseen or covered by the manual, great reliance must be placed upon the application of godly judgment and wisdom by all members of the guard and by all watchmen. In situations not covered by this manual and where doubt arises as to the proper action to be taken, the guard must consider the mission assigned to him/her and apply godly judgment in praying the required and mandated prayer.

The material in this manual is applicable to Spiritual warfare and physical or natural warfare.

THE WATCHMAN CREED

I am a watchman on the wall. I am appointed by GOD.

I take my assignment seriously, for I am the early warning system for the Body of Christ.

I neither sleep nor slumber while on duty. I pray without ceasing. I seek God and wait   patiently for HIS answer.

I have no opinion or personal precepts or hidden agendas when it comes to interceding.

I pray the Holy Scriptures with conviction. I confess the Word over sins or situations.

I proclaim God's word in Victory. I declare God's Favor; His Will.
I believe God's Word.

I speak God's Word in a positive life-giving manner. I give HIM thanksgiving even before HE answers prayers.

I will not be intimidated by tactics used by the enemy.

I will dismantle, destroy, and disconnect ALL demonic plots set out against me, and those assigned to me!

I speak the TRUTH in love and will not use my words against another watchman or those assigned to me.

I intercede with expectancy; not wavering or doubting.

I will not lose heart or faith in what I know God is able to do.

All my prayers are sealed in Jesus's Holy Name and with a hearty **Amen!**

SOUND THE ALARM!

Just like an alarm clock wakes you up in the natural; God has been waking his people up in the spiritual. Some of his people are still asleep. Some hit the snooze button and some just refuse to get up. The sound has alerted God's watchmen, intercessors, and prayer warriors. It's time to pray, seek God's face, study the Bible like never before. Some are going to be shocked for what's going to take place because they have chosen to not hear God or the message of his watchmen. Not listening causes spiritual casualties.

The sound is designed to inform God's people that it's time to pray, seek HIM, get into HIS word like never before. The bride of Christ is not ready for the events that are about to take place. God has been warning us; but some has missed it or have chosen to be ignorant of what's going on. The enemy has many blinded. The enemy may be busy but God still is on the throne and HE's doing more than what the enemy could ever do.

Daniel 3
King Nebuchadnezzar sound an alarm that he wanted at a certain time of the day all people, nations, and languages to worship an image that he had made and the people were supposed to accept it.

People often hear different things when an alarm sounds. Some hear a wake-up call to pray, some hear it's time for them to get up and go to work (evangelism going after souls) and some hear it's time to fast. When the alarm sounded, you knew the enemy was ahead or near. All that has been going on with God's people is to call them to pray. Whenever my people pray, it brings change around the world, in their communities, from the President to their individual houses. The Lord has strategically placed his intercessors (guards) in certain areas and they will speak what they hear God say. God has put them in a place where they will be uncompromising.

The next time that you hear the alarm, what will you choose to do?

PART ONE

Understanding What Spiritual Guard Duty is all about

1

TERMINOLOGY

The terminology relative to guard duty listed below has derived from both a military manual on guard duty (FM 22-6) and the Bible in several versions or translations.

Watch—to pray; to be on guard; to intercede or look out

Watchman-(Sentinel) A guard or sentry stationed at city gates. These watchmen also patrolled the streets and called out the hours of the night.[1] (2 Samuel 18:24-27)

Guard-A soldier who provides personal protection for a ruler; a body guard (2 Chron. 12:11)

> *"And when the king entered into the house of the Lord, the guard came and fetched them and brought them again into the guard chamber.*
>
> 2 Chron. 12:11

Commander or Chief of the Guard (FM 22-6) He's the senior officer of the guard. He is responsible for the instruction, discipline, equipment, and performance of the guard.

> *"So King Rehoboam made bronze shields to take their place and gave them to the commanders (chiefs) of the guards for the palace gates."*
>
> 2 Chron. 12:10 NCV

In our day, this is the leader placed over the Prayer Ministry or Intercessory Team. The chief of the guard was responsible to carry the shields and to protect the king wherever he went. The guards carried the shields whenever the king was to enter the temple of the Lord. The Intercessory Team or Prayer Ministry are the guards put in place to protect the interest of, First and Foremost our King Jesus Christ and undergird the vision of the Pastor. The chief of the guard receives the mandates from both Heaven and the Pastor, give the intercessors under their authority, and care those prayer mandates.

Guard (FM 22-6) definition- (1) a special unit responsible to the Officer of the day for the protection and security of an installation or area. (2) An individual responsible to keep WATCH over, protect, shield, defend, and warn or any duties prescribed by General Orders and Special Orders. Also referred to as a Sentinel, Sentry, or lookout.

    Guards Post- An area for which the guard is responsible. Within his/her post, a guard performs the duties required by his/her General Orders and Special Orders.

    Spiritually we are assigned an anointing, mantle, calling, or office in which we operate. Some intercede for the global needs of the church; some intercede for certain nations, some for healing, some for leadership, and so forth. There is a specific "post" or "assignment" assigned to individual intercessors and intercessory teams. God (Commander) usually mandates these to the Officer of the Day (Pastors) for their Chiefs of the Guard (Intercessory Leaders). Some call these "Prayer Targets"; but they are <u>Orders</u>.

Commanding Officer (GOD) God is the ONLY one who can appoint and commission guards (intercessors). There is a difference between praying and interceding and we will cover that later in the book.

Field Officer of the Day (Pastors) an official selected to be the personal representative or liaison of the Commanding Officer. The Pastor receives all instructions from God and passes the information down to the commanders or chiefs of the guard. Guards (Intercessors) need to be careful when praying in a corporate setting that they are NOT praying against the mandates or "Prayer Targets." There may be times when the Spirit unction an intercessor to pray specifically for a need or concerned; but it should still fall in line with the prescribed mandate.

Guardhouse-A building, tent, or specific location occupied by guards appointed as "interior" guards (meaning they pray inside the temple). The guardhouse is the place where guards gather to pray. Interior guards are assigned to secure the inside of a place and pray for the ministry. Exterior guards guard the outside and are not assigned to a specific ministry, but rather to a region, community, or group of people who may not be members of the ministry in which they are part of. Most exterior guards work in outreach or soul winning. They are the ones sent to cover the exterior of an installation or organization.

Correctional Officer- Appointed by the Commanding Officer (God) and is charged with the custody, administration, and treatment of prisoners (sinners, those bound by any sin or spirit). This person's heart is for those in bondage. They intercede with great devotion for those whom the Father releases into their care. These are also your designated Altar workers because they have a heart for deliverance and know how to cast out demonic spirits.

Challenge—any process carried out by the guard in efforts to identify if the Spirit is friendly or hostile in character. This is a way of spiritually discerning if what you are dealing with is of a demonic nature. For the military, a simple command: "Halt, who goes there?" inviting the approaching party to identify itself. For us in the Spirit we pray: "Father, reveal to us the real Spirit in Operation."

Spirit—A word which denotes man's reason, conscience, and nobler affections (2 Cor. 7:1, Ephe. 4:23) in contrast to our soul—our appetites, passions, and sensations. The root word of the word "wind" (John 3:8)

Spirits in Prison- (1 Pet. 3:18-20) Christ in HIS spiritual existence, preached to "Spirits in Prison" who disobeyed God during the days of Noah. Some scholars claim that Christ did not descend into Hell but that HIS eternal spirit (which later were made alive in HIS resurrection) preached to the spirits at the time of their disobedience.

Familiar Spirit-The Spirit of a dead person which a sorcerer calls up in order to communicate with that person—(Deut. 18:11) The Spirit of Samuel was called up by a witch (I Sam. 28: 3-20) such sorcery was considered an abomination by God.

Password—The word of God that is the only acceptable reply to a challenge. God's Word is our light.

Parole—A special (prophetic word) used to confirm the password (or word) uttered at a gathering or prayer meeting. The prophetic word has to line up with the Word of God and the dates/times we live in. It will always be confirmed by or to the chief of the Guard or other guards.

2

GUARD COMPOSITION

In this chapter we will be discussing the composition of the guard i.e. intercessory team. We will define the role of each type of guard.

Interior Guard
They are appointed by God, confirmed by Pastors to protect and enforce the regulations and mandates of said organization. These intercessors are selected by God and the Pastor to intercede continually over their assigned ministries and over the mandates for such ministry. They are privy to information not known to the congregation or to the public. The Pastors and Intercessory Team leaders must ensure that the "intercessors" are trained properly, qualified or familiar with the weapon they use on guard. Prayer is our weapon of choice. We train in the area of having a strong prayer life and study life. Application is what qualifies us to be intercessors or guards. A great intercessor or guard is not ONE who may know just what to say or has the prayer vernacular memorized; but the ONE who lives a life of prayer and is evident or shows in their everyday walk and treatment of others especially those of the household of faith. (2 Tim. 2:15, I Thes. 5:17)

The Main Guard
The main guard consists of a combination of patrols and fixed posts. This is why you see intercessors kneeling, prostrated (lying down) or walking around praying or waving banners of worship.

Exterior Guard
They are not formal or restricted as the interior guard. These are the ONES in the trenches on the battlefields. They are set as lookouts, listening posts, out posts, specifically designated patrols, and guards in combat zones, field-training areas, and guards outside the limits of a particular ministry. These are global intercessors. They intercede on a global scale. The mandates for these intercessors are not limited or confine to their "ministry" or "individual" life; but they are called to be prophets to the nations. Exterior guards still perform their duties as prescribed by special orders and instructions. They are still subject to the leadership—but they are mostly needed out in the communities; regions; nations.

Gate Guard
The gate guard should not allow anyone to come in and out of the gate. The gate is always to remain close until access is granted. In the spiritual realm, there are gates that serve as entry points for demonic spirits. The gate guard has prophetic insight allowing him/her to see what demonic spirit is in operation and trying to gain access into our camp. In the natural, before anyone is welcome into the courts (church, our lives) the gate guards know who is expected to come by the king. All visitors are announced before entering into through the gate. Identification is imminent. We always have to identify what and who is trying to come in through the gates. This prevents "secret" attacks. When you know what's in your midst; you can combat it properly.

Roaming Guard
The roaming guards are free to move around the perimeter. They walk throughout the sanctuary praying. They may also walk the

streets praying. Since the gate guards cannot leave their post (assignment); the roaming guard is there to help the gate guards. Their job is to ensure that there are no secret attacks. The roaming guard has more visibility than the gate guard does; but they are still subject to the information given to them by the Commander(s) of the Guard (Intercessory Team Leaders). They also are alert and know how to warn the leaders of any attack or possible attacks by the enemy. Because they roam around the perimeter, they get a sense of what the other prayer warriors and guards are doing. When sin, negative plots, and different demonic spirits enter into the camp, they know how to touch heaven and cancel the demonic assignments. The roaming guard is fully aware of what is going on around them. They may not always address the problem with the individual(s); but through wisdom, fasting, and praying they connect spiritually or are in tune with their leaders.

The Watchman
The watchman sits in the tower or observation points. He/she has the best position in the perimeter or camp to be able to see from afar the enemy and stop him on his tracks. These guards are the "seers" of the camp. These guards are a great asset to the other guards. The watchman is aware of everything that is going on both near and far because they see things before it happens. These people alert or inform the people of God for potential danger ahead. Once the alarm has sounded, it is up to the people to know what they will do with the information. When the intercessors (guards) are not properly on their posts; working outside of their lane (calling); or are found doing the wrong thing, we end up having spiritual casualties because the camp has been infiltrated or overran by the enemy. Spiritual casualties can be avoided if the guards are properly posted and are alert.
   Don't be caught sleeping on Guard Duty!!

3

GENERAL ORDERS

"...Appointed by God."

Ezekiel 3:7

General Order Number One

I will guard everything within the limits of my post and ONLY quit my post when properly relieved.

> *"...And I sent messengers unto them saying, I am doing a GREAT work, so that I cannot come down: why should the work cease whilst I leave it and come down to you?"*
>
> Nehemiah 6:3 (KJV)

"Pray without ceasing."

I Thessalonians 5:17

Post- An area of prayer assigned to either the Intercessor by the Commander (God) or the Field Officer of the Day (Pastor). The Commander of the Relief or Guard (Intercessory Team Leader) may also assign areas of interests or "prayer targets" for each individual intercessor. What this does is give each intercessor a sense of responsibility and purpose. The gifted intercessor may be gifted in specific areas. For example, in studying Ezekiel, I noticed God dealt with him through visions. Ezekiel also experienced being "translated" to different areas in order for God to show him what he should intercede for. You may have an intercessor on your team who sees and understands visions. It is good to assign to them any vision seen by any member of the team for him/her to pray over it. These posts (areas of responsibilities) are not to be quit by the intercessor until they are properly relieved.

What does it means to be properly relieved? Who can relieve you? As intercessors we have mandates given to us by 1) God, 2) Our leaders and 3) Our Personal Mantles or Anointing. (We will discuss "mantles" later)

So, we are properly relieved when we have: 1) A praise report, 2) When God has released us from the assignment or 3) when our Pastors have changed the mandates or targets. Intercessors do not cease or quit their "posts" until God, their leaders, properly relieves them or there has been a praise report.

General Order Number 2
I will obey my Special Orders and perform all my duties in a Christian (Watchman) manner.

> "Obey them that have the rule over you and submit yourselves: for they watch for your souls, as they must give account, that they may do it with joy and not with grief: for that is unprofitable for you."
>
> Hebrew 13:17

When on guard duty, you will be given Special Orders or instructions by your leaders i.e. Pastors or Team Leaders. You must obey those Special Orders. A life of submission and obedience is the life of the watchman or intercessor. If you have an issue with obeying or submitting to leadership may be you are not ready to be part of the Intercessory Team.

We obey the Special orders because we are the ministry's first line of protection. That's why we are set on the walls so that if we see anything far off, we can warn the rest or veer off the attack. We ought to be "watchful" (Prayerful) and alert (not easily distracted) because we see what's coming and we guard against it. Our Pastors they should be men/women of God who sees the danger and give us what to pray for or against. Pastors have prophetic insight as well.

When they instruct us, on what to pray or intercede; we obey and submit. We then do it or perform it in a Christian manner. This can mean many things, but as far as "Intercession" is concerned, it means we pray the scriptures. We do not pray vague and empty prayers. The Word of God has Dunamis power and all we have to do is send it out (like throwing spears or shooting arrows) at our enemies or prayer targets.

Again, emphasis is on the fact that you (intercessor) must be properly trained on your assigned weapon. You have to know how to properly pray and we will discuss this when we get into the different prayer modules.

General Order Number 3
I will report violations of my special orders, emergencies, and anything not covered in my instructions to the Commander of the Relief (Intercessory Team Leader).

> "Son of man, I have made thee a watchman unto the house of Israel: therefore heart the word of my mouth, and give them warning from me."
>
> Ezekiel 3:17 KJV

Watchmen "watch"—they sit upon the Wall (position of visibility) and they watch (pray). The sole purpose of us "watching" is to see what's coming and to be able to warn others. Watchmen are the early warning system of the body of Christ. They may see or hear things before anyone else. We are admonished to report these things to the I-team Leaders and they will report it to the Pastor. Once you have report it—the blood will no longer be required at your hands, even if they decide not to report it to the Pastor. The military calls this "chain of custody". You have given custody of what God has given you or shown you to the leaders and it is up to them to be spiritual enough to see what's being reported and warn the body. There may be times where what you may report may not be considered a violation of your special orders; or an emergency; so they may pray over it and wait for God to prompt them to either report it or disregard it. At which point, they may or may not let you know.

Violation of Special Orders
If your prayer target is to pray for healing for a particular member and God shows you that he/she needs to be delivered from something before they can receive their healing i.e. may be the request for was for liver condition but the person is still drinking. This has to be brought up or reported to the Intercessory Leaders.

Maybe you have been assigned to pray for a business transaction to take place between the church and a vendor—but God shows you this vendor is a thief or an exploiter. You research the internet and find facts to support it. You have to report it.

If what you are being asked to pray for doesn't line up with God's word. Report it.

Emergencies
Pray requests that are not mandated by the leaders; but present imminent danger or need. Such as death of a loved one or member, accident, disaster, etc.

Anything Not Covered
If your special orders or prayer targets for the month is to pray for new disciples; but God shows you to pray for the leaders---then you report it.

Personal Interests
This may be areas that you are "used" to or "comfortable" with interceding. For example, a person with an intercession anointing of Daniel—maybe interested or comfortable praying for nations, leaders, and governments. He/she may be prophetically seeing what is happening with world leaders. This may be an area that they are most comfortable praying for. Also, if you have mandates for your own life. These will be personal interests.

It is okay to pray for these things; but after you have prayed for the targets assigned to you. Think of yourself as a hired "hitman." You are hired (appointed) to seek and go after specific "targets." If you miss or abort the mission it may result in you getting in a lot of trouble with those that hired (appointed) you or making a bigger mess. You do not want to deviate from the prayer targets assigned to you. They are important and do require your immediate attention.

4

GUARD SHIFTS/PRAYER WATCHES

Why is it important to have shifts or watches?

It is a strategy used to protect the perimeter or theater (military terms for post) and in the spiritual it deals with what you should be "watching" (praying; guarding; interceding) for or against.

Guards (watchmen, intercessors, prayer warriors) are any ministry's first line of protection. They see what is coming and they through the Holy Spirit's leadership know what to pray for (Romans 8:26…*we do not know what we ought to pray for; but the spirit himself intercedes for us through wordless groans.*" It is imperative that as intercessors we learn how to depend on the Holy Spirit and lean on HIM when we may not be clear on what or how to pray concerning an individual, spirit in operation, or circumstance.

Watches or shifts are also designed to give the intercessors rest. Guards are assigned to different watches or shifts. The shifts were sometimes divided in increments of 2 hours shifts with two guards assigned, three hours shifts with one to four guards assigned, or four hours shifts with four to six guards assigned. It is all dependent on the size of the perimeter and what the Commander of Relief has received as instructions from the Commanding Officer and the Field Officer (God or the Pastor).

The mandates that God downloads to his leaders play a very important part in how and what we guard and watch against. The prayer targets that ware assigned to us by the Intercessory Team Leaders often comes from the Pastor or Higher echelon. (God, Bishops, Apostles). Sometimes, we tend to mix our own personal prayer targets with the ones given to us by our leaders. This should not be. Your prayer targets are done on your personal time in between shifts (watches). While on duty on your post, your focus is the prayer targets assigned to you by God and your leaders.

Submission to your General and Special orders is vital to the kind of prayer life that you will have.

Now let's explore some of the watches.

When I first was led by the Spirit of God to do a "prayer fast" back in 2009, HE instructed me to assign people to different "shifts" or "watches." He gave me these shifts according to the biblical numeral meaning of each number.

- 3- Deals with the divinity or divine assignments and appointments.
- 6- deals with mankind and its needs
- 9- deals with judgment, discipline or lack there of
- 12- Deals with government, discipleship, order.

The Spirit had me praying at each hour. I would get up and pray at 6:00 am for mankind because six is the number of man. Man was created on the 6th day. (Genesis 1:24-31) From that instruction, I would pray again at 9:00 am. I would pray for finality and judgment against wicked nations. For divine intervention of God against injustice and so forth. At 12:00 pm, I would pray for our government, our leaders, for our churches, and for new disciples. At 3:00 pm, I would pray for divine assignments, appointments, and for God's divine will. I would pray for the Holy Trinity to be accepted and followed. I would do this around the clock. Sometimes the Holy Spirit would instruct me or give me details on specific targets—but it would still fall in line with the biblical value of the number. That is only one way the watches work.

Steve Brook has another way to break down the watches. His are also biblical in reference. He calls them "prayer watches" and they are eight (new beginning; fresh anointing). Every shift has a different anointing assigned to it.

6pm to 9pm the Evening Watch
Reference Scriptures: Matt. 14:28—Jesus seeding into your future/sowing into your tomorrow. (Notice its still prayers dealing with man number six)

9pm to Midnight the Night Watch
Psalms 119:148—King David---*"My eyes are wide awake through the night watches, that I may meditate on your word."* People who lean into this prayer watch—many experience translation later at night. (Phillip, Elijah, Ezekiel) It can also take place when you are asleep. The mind and body needs rest, but the spirit does not need rest. If you go into the night season prayed up, you are primed for translation. (Being taken to another place either by vision or dream)

Midnight to three am the Third Watch
Also called "The Lonely Watch", this is the time when God sends out HIS special forces. Divine anointing on this time for setting prisoners free. Acts 16:25, Paul and Silas were praying together—in prison, and they were set free. This is also the type of prayer that would release people out of things that they cannot get out unless you go into intercessory prayer. Set people free. The enemy is slain at night. God will give you HIS best. He will send mighty angels to stand with you. Warring angels are different than regular angels. According to Steven Brooks, during a time of fasting, he had a vision and he saw the warring angel who was alert and in position. And another warring angel came in looking sharp and fresh and relieved the angel

that had been with Steven for the last three years (that warring angel had grey hair and looked tired, but the angel who relieved him had black hair and looked refreshed.)

*If we do not pray, there are people who will literally die and go to Hell. Warring angels are assigned to us to keep us alert and prayerful.

3am to 6am the Fourth Watch (Mystery Realm Watch)
Some people start this watch at 2:30 am because they want the best of both realms. This is when your body is in its deepest sleep. Over 90 percent of Steven Brooks' dreams happened just before he wakes up. It happens to me in the same way. (Matt. 14:25) In the fourth watch, Jesus walked on the water. The anointing associated with this watch is one of intimacy and closeness with Jesus. It also has to do with your walk with HIM. What will this level of anointing do in your life? And in your walk with the LORD? For Peter, it caused him to walk on water as the Lord. It requires focus and trust. Peter was able to stay on top of the water as long as his focus was on JESUS. We have to be focused to be able to command the mornings and the dawn as the Lord instructed Job to do. (Job 38:12).

Tremendously spiritual activity going on between angels and demons during this time of the morning.

6 am to 9 am- The Fifth Watch (Morning Watch or Equipping Time)
This is the time where you get ready for the day. Where you receive your instructions for the day. It is also the time of day where a down pouring of God's Spirit happens so that the watchmen are equipped for the shift. Some of us loved this shift because it doesn't mess up our daily routines. It was the one that once we were relieved from this shift, we would have the rest of the day and night to rest.

9am to Noon - The Sixth Watch
Practice the Lord's presence and pray without ceasing.

Noon to 3pm- The Seventh Watch
This is the prayer watch for the protection of loved ones. You can intercede for those who God lays on your heart. There's an anointing to go under the shadow of HIS wings at 1:00 pm or 2:00 pm.

3 pm to 6 pm- The Eighth Watch
There's an anointing on this watch—close of business day. At 3 pm, the Lord said "It is finished." This is the time to ask God for something special including spiritual gifts. [1]

The overall goal of the "watches" or "shifts" is to have intercessory prayer going on 24 hours a day, so that the intercessors are not sleeping or resting; but on their post. It also promotes spiritual awareness and growth. It is mandated that you assign each intercessor(s) according to their prophetic mantle, anointing, or insight. In most cases, intercessors will operate in the gift of prophecy. Rotating the guards give each guard a chance to experience praying at different times of the day and under different anointing. Don't allow or give room for "weariness" or "fatigue." Remember that even the warring angels in the man of God's vision got properly relieved. You don't want to be worn out or to wear out your team.

One of the key elements when building up your intercessory team is that through discernment you select people who are disciplined. The life of a watchman is a life of discipline. Sometimes the discipline is strict as in the case of Ezekiel who wasn't even allowed to mourn for his wife nor bury her. A watchman must stray in his/her assignment until they are relieved by God. Other intercessors were in captivity while interceding for the people of God: Jeremiah, Daniel, Ezekiel, and Paul to name a few.

Don't think that your situation or circumstances change your assignment, because it doesn't. Watchmen are vigilant; there's no sleeping on the job! Watchmen are relentless; they can't stop won't stop. They are persistent.

The times for the watches do not change. They are always done at 3, 6, 9, and 12. However, those are not just the ONLY times to pray. You're admonished to pray without ceasing. (I Thes. 5:17).

Prayer should be as important to you as breathing is. You don't forget to breathe, right? So don't forget to pray. The level of prayer that we are discussing in this book, deals with those who are called beyond the normal "prayer" life into a surrendered, submissive, life of interceding or intercession. There's a difference between prayer and intercession and we will discuss this later when we dissect some, not all, prayer modules by some great men in the bible.

PART TWO

Prayer Modules

Exploring How Some of the Greats Pray

5

PRAYER VS. INTERCESSION

What is Intercession?
n. The action of intervening on behalf of another (arbitration, conciliation, negotiation)

When you go into your prayer closet, you go in there with specific instructions (prayer targets) either from your leaders or directly from God. It is in your prayer closet that you begin to fight someone else's battle. Intercession solely deals with praying for someone else in such a way that you've placed yourself between them and God. You, as an intercessor, become the Point of Contact (POC) between God and the person(s) needing intercession. It is important that when you intercede; you do so with a clear mind and heart. You don't want to become a hindrance or an obstacle to someone's answer or deliverance. It's also used as strategic warfare (Eph. 6:12) because our warfare is not a physical one; but a spiritual one.

What is Prayer?
n. A solemn request for help or expression of thanks addressed to God. An earnest hope or wish. [2]

Prayer (in my opinion and experience) is how we communicate with God. We come into HIS presence, with thanksgiving and we make our requests known unto HIM. Prayer can be both personal and regarded as "intercession." However, there's a difference. In one you're fervently pleading for somebody else's needs (Intercession) in the other you may be pleading, or simply thanking God in advance for what He is getting ready to do.

When we ask Amiss?
A 'miss adj.

1. Out of proper order.
2. Not in perfect shape; faulty.

Adv. In an improper, defective, unfortunate, or mistaken way, wrong; incorrect; or faulty.

There's a correct way to pray and we went over the basic elements of prayer as taught by our Lord and Savior. There's also an incorrect (amiss) way of praying. God is a God of order and everything that HE does; He do in *decency* and in order. (I Cor. 14:40) To know the order of God we must be in relationship with HIM. We learn HIS perfect or divine order by studying HIS Son Jesus. Jesus was and is the epitome of order. Even when nailed to the cross; He didn't complain as some of us would. He knew the order of God.

How do we pray amiss?
Well if we know that God has an order, but we pray out of our own will or what we perceive to be right; we are praying from our own lusts and that's amiss. James 4:3 GW explains it as such, "when you pray for things, you don't get them because you want them for the wrong reason—for your **own** pleasure."

Could we be praying amiss when we pray for others to be healed? It may not seem that we are praying amiss when we are praying for someone to be healed; but we may be out of the order of God for that individual's life. We have to pray that God's will be done and accept God's will –even if the end result is the person dying. Harsh as it may seem- sometimes even though we see a loved one suffering from a terminal disease—we want to hold on to them while God's will may be for us to let them go. Intercessors are negotiators but they do so in wisdom. Negotiators know the rules of negotiation. They know what to negotiate for and what's not feasible. We need to know this as well.

…We have not because we ask not or we ask amiss…

[Incorrectly; with faulty motives]. It may also be that we ask for things to fulfill our own fleshly pleasure. There's nothing wrong with wanting a home; a job; a car; or more income. Those are things we obviously need; but when our prayer life is consumed by what we desire or what pleases us rather than what pleases God—we are praying "amiss." We begin to "miss" our prayer targets. Remember that prayers have targets. We don't want to miss our targets. We want to qualify in our assigned weapons by hitting as much targets as we can. That's what's going to get us "experts" or "sharp shooter" with our weapons. We don't want to settle for just "marksman." We desire to be sharp in our prayer life.

We have to know the will of God…

What is the will of God concerning healing? For example: God wants us to prosper in every other way and that our souls are healthy as well. (I John 1:2 emphasis mines) If we are to prosper in health, even as our souls prosper, then we know that God's will is for us to be healthy. So how do we handle not being healthy? Do we get angry at God because we are seeing the symptoms of something that was healed by HIS stripes?

Isaiah 53:5 GW *"He was wounded for our rebellious acts. He was crushed for our sins. He was punished so that we could have peace and we received healing from HIS wounds."* Healing manifested through Christ's wounds. When we experience medical issues in our lives; that could be a direct result of something we have done or just a way for God to get the glory.

What I mean by something that we have done is: if we have smoked cigarettes and drank alcohol for most of our adult life—this may lead to problems with our lungs or liver or worst. This doesn't mean that God willed for this to happen; we did that to our bodies by ingesting chemicals that weren't healthy. But in the case of the bling man (John 9) Jesus explained that although this man was blind from birth, neither the man nor his parents sinned. Instead, he was born blind so that God could show what HE can do for him when HE healed him.

I know what you are thinking what about the ONE who goes blind after he/she was born seeing? Again, nobody sinned. Sometimes there's a bigger purpose to our pain. Bigger than what we may "see" with our natural eyes.

So when interceding; it's imperative that we know the will of God. And even if we don't find HIS will in HIS Holy Word.

In the bible, there are some prayer modules from great men of faith and of battle as in the case with both Abraham and King David, but our Lord, Jesus has established some key elements of prayer.

Prayer Elements from the Lord's Prayer (Matt. 6:5-)

- Don't pray to be "seen" or "recognized." Prayer is done secretly; discreetly; but even in a group setting, it's done in an orderly fashion.

    > "The hypocrites they like to stand in synagogues and on street corners to pray so that everyone can see them."
    >
    > Matthew 6:5

- Don't pray to draw attention to yourself. Over talking or over praying can be a distraction to the guards in your team. Pray quietly and allow for others to pray as well.
- When you pray go to your room and close the door.

Intercession is not public prayer. For Intercessory Teams intercession is not done during the service in the sanctuary. Your secret place is where you battle uninterrupted and without any distractions. You cannot "intercede" for someone in the hustle and bustle of the day; you may can pray; but not interceded. Intercession requires a level of secrecy and strategy that's not always available or accessible during a worship service. Prayer can be done anywhere.

A lot happens behind closed doors. Jesus performed miracles behind closed doors as in the case of the young girl who had died. Prayer happens behind closed doors, in other words, in secret. We don't pray to be seen and when we pray we do it discreetly.

- Pray privately to your Father who is with you.

    "Your father sees what you do in private and rewards you openly."

    Matthew 6:6b

- Avoid rambling or saying a bunch of words that are vague and empty.

    Some people talk just to hear themselves talk and some people pray just to hear themselves pray. The Bible calls them "heathens." Don't be like them.

    "When you pray, don't ramble like heathens who think they will be heard if they talk a lot."

    Matthew 6:7

Be specific; use God's scriptures as your guides and anchors. Don't repeat vain repetitions; thought they may sound "Holy"; they are NOT. But be sincere and honest when you pray.

- Your Father knows what you need before you ask him (Matt. 6:8)

    Again, praying target prayers is the way to go. You stay on target and avoid rambling just for the purpose of sounding "Holy."

    Now you are ready to pray using the elements and fundamentals described by Jesus. If there was one person who knew how to pray—surely it was Jesus Christ our Lord. So let's explore what He mandates for us to do when we pray.

6

THE LORD'S PRAYER
(JESUS'S PRAYER MODULE)

Learning how to intercede from Jesus our Lord and Savior.

Seven Key Elements of Prayer

1. *Acknowledgement-*

    We must acknowledge God the Father before we bombard HIM with our requests and supplications. The salutation of any letter is of key importance and sets the tone for the rest of the letter. In prayer, acknowledging God sets the tone for the rest of the prayer and gets HIS attention.

    "Our Father who art in heaven…"

    Matthew 6:9

2. *Reverence*

    His name is HOLY and should be kept Holy (sacred; separated) Why is this so important? God is a God of order and decency. It is giving HIM honor or reverence. When we come before a judge—we address him/her as "your honor"; we address some leaders as "Your Majesty" or "Your Highness"—this is shown as reverence. We reverence God.

"Hallowed be thy name..."

Matthew 6:9b

3. *Invocation (Inviting HIS Kingdom)*

   "Thy kingdom come..."

   Matthew 6:10

We invoke HIS presence and by doing so, we're invoking or inviting HIS kingdom (His way of doing things to come). We have to be overly concerned about HIS kingdom and the way HE wants things to be done.

"When we seek HIS kingdom first; then all other things will be added (given) unto us."

(Matt. 6:33)

4. *Alignment*

   "Let thy will be done on earth as it is in heaven..."

   Matthew 6:10b

Again, we want HIS kingdom to come to earth. We do so by aligning ourselves to HIS will. Whatever God wants us to do or be; it's HIS will. We need to give access for HIS will to be done in us who are citizens of earth for now. Matthew 18:18 is a principle that comes to mind when we want to align ourselves to HIS will. (*Whatever we imprison, God will imprison and whatever we set free, God will set free...both in heaven and in earth.*)

When we align ourselves with God; we become HIS ally and therefore whatsoever things we pray for if we ask in the name of Jesus—God the Father will do. But we must invoke HIS will.

5. *Provision*

   "*Give us this day our daily bread...*"

   Matthew 6:11

Daily God supplies and gives us our benefits. We invoke HIS provision. We ask for HIS daily bread, His provision not just in the tangible; but in the spiritual as well. We know that HE is a provider and so we need to ask HIM for our daily provision. What we need each day has already been established and provided for—all we need to do is receive it. First ask for it; then receive it.

6. *Forgiveness*

   "*Forgive us our debts as we also forgive our debtors...*"

   Matthew 6:12

Why is forgiveness an element of prayer? Because God will not accept your offering (this can mean your prayer; praise; or actual offering) if you have something against somebody else. Also, the one who has been forgiven the most is the one who forgives much. We don't want anything blocking our prayers—unforgiveness blocks prayers.

So we must forgive others; so that our Heavenly Father can forgive us. (Matt. 6:14-15) Ask for forgiveness; but make sure that you have forgiven others before you ask God to forgive you.

7. *Salvation and Deliverance*

> *"Don't lead us into temptation but deliver us from evil…"*

Matthew 6:13

We need to be saved daily from temptation. Those who say that they don't get tempted are lying. Every day we are tempted. And every day we need to pray that God will rescue or save us from the temptation and deliver us from the evil one: Satan.

Praying In His Name
There's power in the name of Jesus. When we pray in HIS name, we build a connection between what we are praying and God the Father. Jesus is that connection.

> "If you ask me (Jesus) to do something, I will do it."

John 14:14 (GW)

Anything that we ask in HIS name, Jesus will do so that the Father be glorified in the Son. It is so easy to pray prayers that "sound" biblical; but may just be a bunch of words put together; but if we follow the prayer modules left by the Greats; we will not go wrong.

When we pray, we do so in HIS name, why? Jesus acts as a "seal." When you seal a letter, it's done. When we seal a petition in prayer, it's a done deal because we know that anything we ask in HIS name will be a <u>done</u> deal.

Phil. 2:10-11 brings another great aspect of Jesus's name and the power it packs. "That at the name of Jesus every knee should bow of things in Heaven and things in earth, and things under the earth; and that every tongue should confess that Jesus Christ is Lord to the glory of God the Father.

His name brings forth Salvation and Deliverance, which are key elements of prayer.

Our prayers should meet goals or have a goal in mind that God the Father will get the glory. That's our ultimate goal; to glorify the Father. It was Jesus's goal and it should be our goal as well.

What does His name means and does for us?

1. *Restores Us*

    Psalms 23:3—"*He restoreth my soul…he leadeth me in the paths of righteousness for HIS name sake…*"—we are not lost or without hope when we pray and believe in the power of His name.

2. *Reminds Us of Our Purpose*

    We give glory to HIS name—"*Give unto the Lord the glory due unto HIS name; worship the Lord in the beauty of holiness.*" (Ps. 29:2 KJV)

    This needs to be a practice of ours: to give HIM glory. To worship HIM daily!! Our lives should be lives of worship—that's our purpose—we were created to worship HIM. In our prayers, we should give HIM glory!!!

3. *Trust in HIS name*

    "*For our heart shall rejoice in HIM, because we trusted in HIS Holy name.*" The name of the Lord should be our assurance. When we trust in HIM, we know we are in good hands. We should trust our request unto HIM. We pray with conviction knowing that our heavenly Father hears us because we pray in HIS son's name.

4. ***Endures forever***

"*His name shall endure forever; His name shall continue as long as the sun and men shall be blessed in HIM. All nations shall call him blessed." Psalms 72:17 Jesus's* name is perpetual; without ending. When we pray, we want to be blessed in HIM and we want those that we intercede for to be blessed in HIM as well. We pray without ceasing because our prayers should be perpetual; on going without ending. We should be relentless because our enemy is relentless.

5. ***Strong Tower***

Ps. 18:10 KJV "*The name of the Lord is a strong tower; the righteous runneth into it and is safe."* Jesus's name provides safety and strength. We know that anything that we ask in HIS name; He will do it—so we pray in strength and with security. "*His name is a shelter and a strong tower from the enemy." Psalms 61:3*

When we believe in prayer and in its power, we pray boldly with expectancy. Knowing that it's a done deal. We also have to understand HIS will. Understanding God's will for our lives and for HIS people will help us pray without wavering.

Jesus as a Watchman

He watches over his disciples (Luke 22:31-32) *"And the Lord said, Simon, Simon, behold Satan hath desired to have you, that he may sift you as wheat: [32] But I have prayed for thee, that thy faith fail not; and when thou art converted, strengthen thy brethren."*

He is up while HIS people are at rest (Psalms 121:3-4) *"He will not suffer thy foot to be moved; he that keepeth thee will not slumber. [4] Behold, he that keepeth Israel shall neither slumber nor sleep."*

All watchmen are called to pray and there are different levels of intercession. Each watchman sees something differently. Some see the enemy in the fashion of demonic spirits. Some see things in the government. Some see sin. Some see what goes on in the heavenly realm. Each watchman/intercessor is used differently but are equally important. Each watchman has a perimeter (area given to them to intercede) that they guard and watch over but it is important that they know what the spirit is saying to the church.

Jesus taught the "masses," but ministered intimately to his disciples and still away to pray to HIS heavenly Father. We can all learn from him how to properly get an audience with God the Father. One thing is for sure, we cannot intercede surrounded by so much commotion and distraction. Jesus, still away to pray, because he knew he couldn't properly hear HIS Father's voice. We can pray anywhere; but we can't intercede in any place. For intercession to be effective, we have to still away.

Jesus watches over His Word *"So shall my word be that goes forth from my mouth; It shall not return ME void, But it shall accomplish what I please, and it shall prosper in the thing for which I sent it."* (Isaiah 55:11 GW) He ensures that whatever comes out of HIS mouth will hit its target. Jesus doesn't miss. Whatever He speaks over us and to us will happen. He makes sure of that, Jesus watches HIS people *"And the Lord said, Simon! Simon! Indeed, Satan has asked for you, that he may sift you as wheat. ³² But I have prayed for you; that your faith should not fail; and when you have returned to ME, strengthen your brethren."* (Luke 22:31-32 NKJV)

God prayed that HIS people's faith would not fail. This is a confirmation to us that we should be concerned about our brothers and sisters. We should help our brothers and sisters. This is why Jesus sits on the right hand of the Father—to intercede.

The Saints

> *"Watch ye therefore and pray always that ye may be accounted worthy to escape all these things that shall come to pass and to stand before the son of man."*
>
> *(Luke 21:36)*

In this passage, Jesus was talking about what is going to happen (end times). He was informing his saints, the prayer warriors, intercessors, the watchmen to pray and be on guard so we can prepare for the things that will take place. In Luke 22:31-32, He prayed so we can stand and not be focused on the enemy but watching so that we can stand before the son of man. This part of what the Apostle Paul was talking about when he admonished us to *"Fight the good fight of faith."*

We cannot be weak soldiers on guard duty. There is no way the enemy should come into the camp or take over your territory when Jesus has equipped us.

The Holy Spirit

Jesus never stops praying for us. He sits on the right hand of God and intercede. (Rom. 8:34, Heb. 7:25)

The word interceded according to Merriam-Webster online means: to mediate.

The Holy Spirit mediates for us because we don't know what we ought to pray for (Rom. 8:26) He mediates because as we pray HE searches our hearts so that we the Saints line up with the Will of God when we pray. (Rom. 8:27)

The Holy Spirit groans (Rom. 8:26). This groan means to travail, which is a deeper form of intercession. These can be consider with the same intensity as that of "labor pains." Sometimes we feel pain on behalf of the person(s) we are interceding for. Sometimes it may be in agony. Jeremiah wept for the people of Israel because it seemed like they would not repent. Often, God shows the watchmen so much to where the Holy Spirit will have us warring for people, nations, and governments. You don't have words to say aloud; but your groaning says everything you would like to put in words.

7

THE WEAPONS OF OUR WARFARE
(PAUL'S PRAYER MODULE)

In this chapter, we will study one of my favorite Intercessors in the Bible: the Apostle Paul. Paul breaks down elements of prayer in such a way that we will know how to engage in spiritual warfare and even rely heavily on the Holy Spirit for HIS guidance and leadership.

> "For though we walk in the flesh, we do not war after the flesh: ⁴(for the weapons of our warfare are not carnal; but mighty through God to the pulling down of strong holds) ⁵ Casting down imaginations, and every high thing that exalteth itself against the knowledge of God, and bringing into captivity every thought to the obedience of Christ;"
>
> 2 Corinthians 10: 3-5

We are going to try to answer these questions:

1. What is warfare?
2. What are weapons (our weapons)?
3. What does it mean to be carnal?
4. What is the result of using your weapons?

The Apostle Paul dealt with the total man; spiritually and naturally. In the above passage of scriptures, Paul was stating that we cannot use human tactics to defeat a spiritual enemy or a principality. Yes, Jesus did pay it all; but when we practice the same tactics as Jesus, God allows us to feel both spiritually and naturally, what victory tastes like. Carnal is doing anything in your flesh where the word of God is not present.

Just like being on guard duty naturally, we are given weapons. Some may be given M16 Riffles, M4, or even a 9 mm handgun depending what or who they are guarding. In the military, we had to first qualify on our assigned weapon before we engage in any type of warfare. Our weapons as the body of Christ are: Word of God. This is why Jesus kept saying in Luke 4th Chapter *"It is written…"* to the enemy. We need the Word. Both the written and the living word (Jesus). Some have Jesus but lack the written and we need both.

Secondly, we must fast: Just like in the military, we train to get us ready for battle. Fasting helps us get ready for warfare. Fasting strengthens us; prepare us for the battle ahead. Through fasting, you spiritually detox and are able to tap into the spiritual realm. There's no such thing as a "surprise" attack in God's Kingdom, especially if you are prayed up and fasting.

Prayer is a key element in every believer's life. We pray the Word because it does not come back to HIM void. The Word helps us to get through the hard times. *He is a very present help in our time of trouble (Psalms 46:1)* the centurion asked Jesus to **speak a word… Heaven and earth shall pass away; but the Word is not going anywhere and one day we shall live together with the Word.**

Praise is also a weapon. There are seven ways to praise when in battle or during warfare.

1. **Yadah (yaw'dah)** To extend your hands as in a way to surrender.
2. **Towdah (to'daw)** This means extending of the hand as when you are giving someone the right hand of fellowship.

3. **Barak (Bar'ak)** Means to kneel in adoration. When the presence of God is strong, we kneel. We kneel in prayer—this is a way we reverence God.
4. **Tehillah (Ta'he'lah)** Means to sing. Before Lucifer fell he was in charge of praise and worship. Anytime true worship is going forth, the enemy cannot stay. The word is **Cretos** meaning to drive the enemy out of your presence. You drive him out with singing; speaking the Word of God and with the clapping of your hands.
5. **Zamar** To pluck the strings of a musical instrument.
6. **Halal** is the primary root word for "praise"...i.e. "**Hal**lelujah" comes from the base word "Halal". It means to be clear, to shine, to boast, to celebrate, and to be clamorously foolish. While some may think that you have lost your mind; sometimes you have to do what you have to do in order to get a break-through.
7. **Shabach** means to shout out loud. When we really need Jesus's attention, we shout his name loudly to know that HE has heard us. This is why we shout at church (the place of worship), at home, in our cars. This shout means that we are in need of something from God.

What is warfare?

1. Engagement in or the activities involved in war or conflict.
2. Spiritual warfare is the same with the addition that you engage in conflicts between what's good and what's evil.

When you are engaged in "warfare", there are some key elements that you must learn and employ.

1. **You must have a plan**- you can't go to war without having a plan. This plan must include knowing who you are fighting. (we will discuss this further)

2. **You must be strategic**-you have to know your enemy and combat him by putting some strategies in place that will do three things: dismantle, destroyed, and dislodge the enemy. You dismantle his plans. You destroy his diabolical assignments and You dislodge or remove by force from his position.
3. **You must have the right equipment**- We need to be equipped for warfare. Warfare requires a totally different mindset; than normal "prayer" or "intercession." In warfare, we don't negotiate with the enemy; we are there to destroy him. We don't plead with him; we command him in the name of Jesus.
4. **You must know the territory of your enemy**- Warfare requires that you familiarize yourself with the battlefield and the area where you will be fighting the enemy. When we fought in the desert, we needed to have gear and equipment that would function in the enemy's territory. You can't fight in a tropical territory with winter gear that you would wear or use if the fight was in Russia or another cold-climate environment.
5. **You must know your enemy's capabilities and tactics**- If you are to be successful in the battlefield; you must know your enemy me and know how he fights. Learn his tactics. Study his movements. You have to become so acquainted with his devices that you know exactly what he will use in different scenarios.

What are weapons?
We already discussed our weapons; but let's go through them again. We have four main weapons of warfare:

1. Prayer
2. Praise
3. Fasting
4. The Word of God

These weapons, when used correctly, will result in victory over the enemy. We employ these weapons by faith. We have to want to know how to properly engage in spiritual warfare. We have to have a heart for "guarding" and "protecting." We have to be on "watch" literally 24/7. We cannot be slothful or lazy. We have to be energetic when it comes to warring in the spirit. We cannot fight a strong enemy; if we are weary and tired. We need our strength and that comes through fasting. Our weapons as you already know aren't carnal. They are not "flesh and blood" type of weapons. They are not literally "guns" and "rifles" or even "bombs". But they are *mighty to the pulling down of strongholds.* (2 Cor. 10:3-5) These weapons are designed by God to destroy spiritual enemies. You can't shoot a gun at the devil; but you can hit him hard with the Word of God. This is why the Word is like a two-edge sword (Heb.4:12) It cuts the enemy going in and out. It makes sure that when we speak the Word over the enemy; his plots are canceled and his motives dismantled.

What does it means to be Carnal?
To be carnal is to mind the things of the flesh. To be in your feelings as some may say or to be "feeling some type of way…" It also means to go against the things of God. A carnal person doesn't mind the things of the spirit because he/she is led by her own flesh. They also cannot properly engage in spiritual warfare because they aren't properly equipped or trained. In the military, this is the soldier who do not qualifies with his/her assigned weapon or never develops professionally. They stay stagnant. They never get promoted because they cannot handle the responsibility of the next rank. I have seen some very carnal Christians and most are in leadership positions that they cannot handle. If you are carnal and you are a member of the intercessory team you become a handicap to the team because everything that the intercessors engage in is "spiritual" and requires that they be led by the Spirit of the Living God. And if you are carnal, you don't

mind the things of God. A carnal prayer warrior is one that will fail in the battlefield because he/she will not submit to God's authority and will pray charismatic prayers. Prayers that "sound" good; but aren't packing any power. The carnal Christians have a form of godliness but no power. They live a powerless life.

What is the Result of Using our Weapons?
Victory. You will always have victory. You will see the fruit of your warfare. You will not be warring for nothing. It will always result in a win-win for us.

8

DANIEL'S PRAYER MODULE

Daniel's Prayer Life

Daniel's prayer life included "fasting." (Dan. 1:8) Daniel had a made up mind not to harm himself by eating the King's rich foods and drinking the King's wine. So sobriety and healthy eating contributed to Daniel living a prayer-focused life.

Dan. 1:17- God gave Daniel and his three friends three things:

1. Knowledge
2. Wisdom
3. Ability to understand all kinds of literature

Daniel could understand dreams and visions. No one was like Daniel and his friends. They were wiser than any other person in the King's court. They prayed and fasted before they gave any interpretation of dreams and visions. Fasting and prayer gets you ready to receive from God concerning a matter or issue that you're assigned to intercede for. It's good to get with other intercessors and fast and pray to see what god wants you to receive or even see.

For any successful group of intercessors; it's always good to have set times of fasting during the week or month.

God revealed secrets to Daniel through "visions." Daniel possessed a dual anointing: apostolic and prophetic. His apostolic anointing had to do with why he was assigned to the government and given a government position because he was to oversee or watch over the kingdom. His prophetic was engrafted in intercession and interpretation of dreams and visions.

Example of one of Daniel's Prayer

> *"Praise God's name from everlasting to everlasting because HE is wise and powerful. He changes times and periods of history. He removes Kings and establishes them. He gives wisdom to those who are wise and knowledge to those who have insight. He reveals deeply hidden things. He knows what is in the dark, and light lives with HIM. God of my ancestors, I thank and praise you. You gave me wisdom and power. You told me the answer to our question. You told us what the king wants to know."*

Daniel 2: 20-23 GW

This was a prayer of intercession for the interpretation of dreams and visions. Daniel's life was full of worship and dedication. He was uncompromising. His three friends were faithful to God and wouldn't compromise. (Dan. 3)

As an intercessor (a guard; watchman), you must not compromise in any shape or form. When guards compromise; they bring danger into their camps. Guards do not give away their positions. This is why on guard duty you weren't allow to bring things that would distract your focus or compromise your position.

Shadrach, Meshach, and Abednego would not compromise their position. (Dan. 3:17) Even when being questioned by the king himself, these brothers weren't budging. I love the response they gave the king: *"If our God, whom we honor, can save us from a blazing furnace and from your power, He will, your majesty, but if he doesn't, you should know, your majesty, we will never honor your gods or worship the gold statute that you set up."*

These three young men were bold and uncompromising; but notice that they were not disrespectful. They honor Nebuchadnezzar by calling him "your majesty"; yet they stood firm in who their God was and what God was able to do; but even if God decided not to deliver them, they would still worship God. This is the attitude that we must have as intercessors. That even if God's answer is different than what we're interceding for, we will still worship HIM.

An attitude of praise and worship is needed to become a successful intercessor.

When you have an attitude of praise and true worship and when you're uncompromising in your stance—Jesus unites with you and HE delivers you from any fiery furnace. (Dan. 3:25)

Intercession invokes promotion. The three Hebrew young men were promoted. (Dan. 3:30)

Daniel prayed three times a day with the windows opened. This was his custom [habit] and no decree from any king was going to change that. An intercessor is dedicated to a life of prayer. He/she is not fearful of what anyone in authority may say to keep them from praying. Of course, we do things in decency and in order, but our prayer life doesn't change because of what others may say or may be doing. Staying true to your calling as an intercessor is detrimental in these last days. We can't be weak or flaky when it comes to intercession. This is why God appoints "watchmen" because someone has to be on guard, on the wall, watching and ensuring the enemy won't come and infiltrate the camp.

Your dedication to being an intercessor (guard) renders you favor with kings and rulers. (Dan. 6:16) The kind knew he had to throw

Daniel into the Lion's den; but he hoped that Daniel's God would deliver him. And God did. Then the king set up a decree for nations and provinces to worship Daniel's God. God dealt with Daniel through prophetic dreams and visions. There are times when God will wake you up and instruct you to pray. There are times when the dreams and visions are areas that HE wants you to intercede in. But this will not happen, if you're not on-guard or have been appointed to watch. When you're literally "watching", you are gaining important information. During these "watches", God downloads intel needed for us to properly counteract the enemy's plots.

Daniel was given visions for us living today. How awesome is that? As an intercessor, you may be given prophetic insight for events that will not happen in your lifetime; but they will happen.

9

PAUL'S PRAYER MODULE (PART 2)

One of the most influential people of the New Testament was the Apostle Paul. His prayer life brought change. He ministered to the whole person and not just certain areas. God had to literally "transform" Paul in order to get him to become one of his absolute MVPs of Bible. Three things were key in Paul's transformation from a blind Saul to an inspiring Apostle Paul:

1. Spiritual eyes open.
2. Filled with the Holy Spirit.
3. He got baptized.

During the three days that he was in Damascus, he received spiritual insight and strength to do God's will. When Paul prayed change came about immediately. (Acts 9:1-7)

After we pray, we should see change within three days. Those that see (watch) know when change is about to take place. They also see where the people are in their walk with God. God answers Paul's prayers immediately. God gave him spiritual sight before natural sight. It should not take us long to do what God has put in us to do. The anointing comes after the laying of the hands. Paul was not struggling in his calling and he was not trying to figure out who he was. He was secured in who God called him to be and was dedicated to his mission. After he accepted his calling and was transformed, deliverance came about. Those who continue in the same mess year after year have not received the Word of God and has not allowed for change to come.

What made the Apostle Paul effective in ministry after he was called was that he didn't allow these three things to hinder him:

1. Acceptance from people.
2. People approval.
3. Seeking attention.

After you pray, it should not take long for God to speak or for you to get an answer and move. There is no reason to stay in the same mess or see no change after three days. Jesus rose on the 3rd day, Paul received sight on the 3rd day, and a believer must get out of that situation on the 3rd day. We should not prolong our trials. But what happens if the deliverance or answer doesn't come as quickly for us as it did for Paul? He stated for us to pray without ceasing because it is our fervent and persistent, along with faith that moves the heart of God. We mustn't stop praying just because there's a delay in the answer. Delay is not denial by any means. Sometimes it is the condition of our heart that delays the answers to our prayers.

Paul was on his way to pray when he was faced with a woman with the spirit of divination. (Acts 16:16-18). Paul was not just prayed up but he was on his way to prayer when he commanded that spirit in the name of Jesus to be cast out of the woman. If you, as a watchman, intercessor, guard, prayer warrior, cannot identify a "spirit", you must check your relationship with Christ. As intercessor we must always know what type of spirit is in operation so that we can properly combat it. When a child of God is faced with all types of spirits; we don't wrestle with them. Jesus did not, Paul did not, and neither should we. We simply must command them to be cast out in the name of Jesus. Our power is in the name of Jesus. His name is the endorsement for us to get the job done. We must not be scared to use the name of Jesus. The name of Jesus is greater and more powerful than any devil you will ever face.

Another thing about Paul's prayer life, it addressed sin head-on. He also encouraged the people working under him to live right and to follow him as he followed Christ. Some of the issues or sins that Paul addressed in his many epistles (letters that included prayers) were:

1. Spiritual Gifts-how to use them for the glory of God
2. How to be equipped in your gifts and callings
3. Revelational knowledge of who Christ really is
4. Being blameless before God
5. Praying without Ceasing
6. No divisions among the brethren
7. Being perfectly joined together in same mind and in the same judgment
8. Contentions
9. Carnality
10. Sexual sin and misconduct
11. Praying in the Spirit
12. Homosexuality
13. Anti-Christ
14. Envy and strife and anything carnal
15. Discipleship effectiveness
16. Studying God's Word
17. Being Fearless

And so much more. I absolutely love Paul's boldness and how he truly cared for his fellow workers in the Gospel. He gave honor where honor was due. He admonished us to pray without ceasing and to allow the Holy Spirit to guide us in prayer. He encouraged the leadership of every church that he was overseeing. He didn't seek for financial assistance or gain, but was grateful for those who contribute to his ministry. Even a jail cell couldn't contain what God had placed inside of Paul!

His message of deliverance was quite clear when he taught us to crucify the works of the flesh. There's so much that can be said about Paul, but one of my favorite prayer is founded in an epistle he wrote to the Ephesians.

Examples of Paul's Prayers, Declarations, and Exhortations

> *"For this reason I bow my knees to the Father of our Lord Jesus Christ, from whom the whole family in heaven and earth is named, that He would grant you according to the riches of His glory, to be strengthened with might through His Spirit in the inner man, that Christ may dwell in your hearts through faith; that you being rooted and grounded in love may be able to comprehend with all the saints what is the width and length and depth and height to know the love of Christ which passes knowledge; that you may be filled with all the fullness of God. Now unto HIM who is able to do exceedingly, abundantly above all that we ask or think, according to the power that works in us, to HIM be glory in the church by Christ Jesus to all generations, forever and ever. Amen."*
>
> (Ephesians 3:14-21)

When Paul wrote to each church (body of believers); he prayed specific prayers. He knew what the church (place of worship) needed and the area(s) where they needed growth in.

Ephesians Believers

- They needed the spirit of wisdom and revelation in the knowledge of Christ
- The eyes of their understanding to be enlightened
- To know the hope of HIS calling and what riches of the glory of HIS inheritance in the saints. (Eph. 2:17-19)

Philippians

- The love of Christ to abound more in knowledge and in all judgment
- Approve things that are excellent
- Be sincere and without offense
- Be filled with the fruits of righteousness (Phi. 1:9-11)

Colossians

- They needed to be filled with the knowledge of his will in all wisdom and spiritual understanding
- Walk worthy of the Lord unto all pleasing, being fruitful in every good work, and increasing in the knowledge of God
- To be strengthened with all might, according to his glorious power unto all patience and longsuffering with joyfulness (Col. 1:9-11)

Thessalonians

- They are to continue to be an example to all believers not just in word but in faith
- They are to continue having patience of hope in our Lord Jesus Christ
- They have received the word in much affliction with joy of the Holy Spirit

- They sounded the word of the Lord in Macedonia and Achaia, but in every place
- They turned from serving idols to serving the Living and True God (I Thes. 1:2-10)

2 Thessalonians 3
Paul's Request for Prayer

- The word have free course and be glorified
- To be delivered from unreasonable and wicked men

Leaders often have prayer requests concerning the work of the Lord that they are embarking upon. A good leader knows how to ask for prayer when he/she feels as though their faith is failing.

Philemon 1:4-7
This was a prayer of a good report.

> *"I thank my God, making mention of you always in my prayers, hearing of your love and faith which you have toward the Lord Jesus and toward all the saints, that the sharing of your faith may become effective by the acknowledgement of every good thing which is in you in Christ Jesus. For we have great joy and consolation in your love, because the hearts of the saints have been refreshed by you, brother."*

There are times that as "guards"; watchmen, intercessors, prayer warriors and leaders we pray giving thanks for somebody else's work of love in the vineyard. It's not always about "Us"; sometimes we are thankful for those who labor among us. Paul was a great leader and example to all of us who are intercessors and leaders.

God gave Paul insight on what each church needed. He prayed for them with diligence and grace. Paul made mention to tell the church he ceases not to pray for them. We should always lift each other up in prayer. If you are seeing a church lacking in an area; pray for them just like Paul did. In his prayers he stressed relationship, people to be filled with the knowledge of Christ and spiritual wisdom. Relationship is important and often times where we attend church services relationship is not stressed nor taught.

We become dependent on the Pastor or Apostle and those that does not relationship when things go wrong; they leave the church (place of worship). Once you come into the knowledge of Christ; you won't become so easily offended nor moved by what you see in others.

Some become dependent on everything and everybody; but the ONE who created them. We must pray for the local places where we attend services, our leaders, and those that have fail or you see falling. Paul did not speak ill of anybody. He was honest about their weaknesses, but diligent in interceding for their deliverance.

As a guard, sometimes God may show us so much and it could be disturbing especially if it's about us or someone close to us. But do not give up on others because God has not given up on you.

10

EXPLORING EZEKIEL'S PRAYER MODULE

Prayer Module

Ezekiel was among the exiles in Babylon by the Chebar River. He was a priest, son of Buzi. God dealt with Ezekiel through visions. Ezekiel was bold. God instructed Ezekiel to speak His word whether the people listened or not. Ezekiel was sent to a defiant and rebellious people. He was told to eat God's Word through a vision of a scroll. There was writing on this scroll, front and back. On it were written:

1. Funeral Songs
2. Songs of Mourning
3. Horrible things

God admonished him to eat the scroll and then speak to the people. The scroll tasted sweet as honey in his mouth. Ezekiel had the task for dealing with stubborn and hardheaded people. But God made Ezekiel as stubborn and hardheaded as the people were. The Ezekiel Intercessor is stubborn, hardheaded, and don't mind being the bearer of bad news. Like the Prophet Jeremiah, Ezekiel was at times bitter and angry.

Could it be because of his audience? Sometimes when we are to deliver a prophetic word, word of knowledge, or word of wisdom, our audiences aren't that great. They may behave just as these stubborn and rebellious exiles. Ezekiel was a watchman and he sat for seven days watching the people.

The Appointed Watchman
Ezekiel was appointed by God to be a watchman (one who watches over people; an intercessor; a guard) The watchman listens to what God says and warn the people for God. Blood is required at the watchman's hand if he/she doesn't tell what the Lord says.

If you deliver the message and the people don't turn from their wicked ways; then you as a watchman is saved. If righteous people go astray—God will make them stumble and they will die (spiritually and naturally).

But if the watchman (Intercessor, prophet, pastor) doesn't warn the people; they are the ones who will die because of their sin and the right things that they did will not be remembered. God holds us responsible for their deaths. But if we warn them and they don't listen; they will surely die because they did not listen to the warning of God.

Ezekiel was given direction by God. God always sends you to a place where HE can speak to you. Ezekiel could see God's glory. This in prophetic intercession is called to be translated to another realm while you're praying or interceding.

Ezekiel Prayer Module

- His prayers were based on visions and dealt with wars; destruction of nations, idolatry; and adulterous hearts. (Ezekiel 1, 2, 3)
- He was admonished to feed on the Word of God (Ez. 3:1-8)

- He listened closely to God and takes to heart everything that God spoke to him (Ez. 3:10)
- He was appointed to be a watchman by God (Ez. 3:17)
- His prayers were warnings
- Accountability is the basis for all intercessors
- Getting direction from God to do certain things or go certain places; being translated in the spirit
- Recognizing the glory of God and bowing down immediately in worship
- Dealt with the attacks on Jerusalem
- 390 days he laid on his left side—40 days on his right side for the sins of the people
- Ezekiel maintained a strict diet consisting of wheat, barley, beans, lentils, millet, winter wheat (We call this Ezekiel Bread)
- He ate 8 oz. of food at set times and drank 2/3 of a quart of water at set times as well
- He prophesied to the mountains of Israel and told them that their altars would be destroyed in front of their idols
- Dealt with the adulterous hearts of people lusting after idols
- Disaster, wars, famines and plagues (Ez. 5:11-12)
- One disaster after another….(Ez. 7:5)
- The visions, teachings of priests and the advice of leaders will disappear (Ez. 7:26)
- Ezekiel only spoke when the power and the spirit of the Almighty God came over him

Translated to Another Realm

The Spirit takes you between the earthly and heavenly realms to show you the secret things that leaders and people are doing. A deep relationship with God is what's being reflected by Ezekiel. The Word of the Lord came to HIM. He was careful not to speak unless God instructed HIM.

Intimacy with God will take you places you've never been before during intercession or your quiet time with HIM. God took Ezekiel to places that weren't of this present world to show him what was going to happen to Israel. Most of Ezekiel's prophecies haven't been fulfilled; especially those leading to a third World War.

Relationship Between God and His People
There are times when God sets his face against his people because of their sins and disobedience. In chapter 16 of the book of Ezekiel, God mandates him to tell Jerusalem about their sins; their disgusting acts. God seen Jerusalem when they were still in their own blood (infancy) and He commanded them to live. Yet, they were doing everything they felt grown to do against God. God covers Jerusalem from their nakedness. God gave Jerusalem back her glory but the people became unfaithful and played the part of a prostitute giving what belonged to God to strangers and idols.

Jerusalem sacrificed their sons and daughters and offered them as burnt offerings to idols so God took some of the land that belonged to Israel and gave it to the Palestinians. Jerusalem kept on prostituting herself even though she wasn't getting paid. She did this to spite God. She was compared to an adulterous wife who prefers strangers to her husband. (Ez. 16: 27-32)

Jerusalem was giving gifts to her lover and bribing them. She paid them; but wasn't accepting payment.
All souls belongs to God, Ezekiel knew this first hand. (Ez. 18:4) He was told by God not to bury his wife nor mourn for her. How many of us would have done that?

Here's a prayer nugget: "Your prayer life has to be strong. There's an on-going fight with the prince of this world—But God's Word will stand against him and all of his angels. Pray God's Word—Pray Strong and without ceasing. Don't lose heart—when you begin to lose heart that's when you begin to sink."

11

HOSEA'S PRAYER LIFE

Hosea was the son of Beeri, in the days of Uzziah, Jotham, Ahaz, and Hezekiah kings of Judah and in the days of Jeroboam the son of Joash, king of Israel. (Hosea 1:1)

An intercessor with a Hosea Anointing must be willing to endure for the sake of the Gospel. Hosea was told to marry a prostitute to show how God's committed to his people though they were idolaters. Hosea also had to deal with having to get Gomer, his prostituting wife, from bars where she was laying with other men. The intercessor must have or develop a "tough skin" to be able to deal with some of the not-so-good mandates of God. For instance, when you have to deliver a message of doom instead of hope. Each child that Gomer bore Hosea had a specific judgment attached from the Lord.

1. Jezreel (first born son) dealt with God avenging the blood shed of Jezree on the house of Jehu and bringing an end to the house of Israel
2. Lo-Ruhamah (daughter and second child) meant that God will no longer have mercy on the house of Israel, but he would utterly take them away
3. Lo-Ammi (son) God declared that Israel were no longer HIS people nor was HE their God.

Hosea's prayers of Restoration:

- Where they were told they would not be HIS people; they will be declared the sons of the living God.
- The children of Judah and the children of Israel shall be gathered together
- For the appointment of leadership
- For mercy to be shown to sisters and brothers
- Against adultery
- For setting those who will not repent as dry lands; unproductive
- For the hedge to be thorns for those who will not repent
- For God's people to return to HIM
- For God to uncover the lewdness of his people
- For God's love for Israel although they were idolaters
- For Israel to return to God
- For the redeeming love of God
- Bringing a charge against the inhabitants of the land
- Against swearing, lying, killing, stealing and committing adultery
- Against bloodshed
- Against contentions; especially against those who contend against the priest (pastor) (Hosea 4:4)
- Lack of knowledge of God's people (Hos. 4:6)
- Rejection of God because people have rejected his knowledge
- Changing their glory to shame because they sinned against God (Hos. 4:7)
- Against the spirit of Harlotry (prostitution; sexual immorality) (Hos. 4:11-12)
- Judgment on Israel and Judah (Hos. 5)

There are times when whatever you're mandated to pray against or for; will become your personal message. Hosea lived in an adulterous relationship because Israel was an adulterous nation. Hosea endured having to see his wife have sexual relations with other men and then he having to pay for her freedom in order for Gomer to return back to him. God paid a ransom for us to return to HIM and be HIS people through the blood of His own son: Jesus Christ.

PART THREE

Short and Simple Prayer Starters

Prayer Against Idolatry (Ezekiel 14:6)
Repent and turn from your idols.

"Lord, help the people to turn themselves away from every idol that they have set up in their heart. Turn away their faces from all of their abominations. Repent and turn to serve you with a willing heart. In Jesus's name, Amen."

Surety of Judgment (Ezekiel 14:13)
"Lord, do not cut off the food supply from our country in judgment; but help us to see the error of our ways. Open up our eyes so that instead of pursuing idols and gain, we are pursuing you. Please do not send famine, pestilence, or war upon the land. Spare the lives of those who serve you with pure and clean hearts. In Jesus's name, Amen."

Healing Prayers

Forgiveness and Healing (Psalms 103:3 Gw)
"Lord, thank you for being the ONE who forgives all of my sins and the ONE who heals all of my diseases. Help me to be as forgiving with those who wrong me, as You are with me. In Jesus's name, Amen."

Rescue from the Grave (Psalms 107:20)
"Lord, send your message to heal all of those who have been diagnosed with a terminal disease. Lord, you are the one who can heal and restore to good health. Rescue them from the grave who have been sentenced by man to die prematurely. It is in Jesus's name, we pray, Amen."

Healer of the Brokenhearted (Psalms 147:3)
"Lord, you are the healer of the brokenhearted. You are the one who can bandage our wounds. Heal our hearts and mend our brokenness. Make us whole again so that we can be about the Father's business and complete the work that you have assigned to us. In Jesus's name, Amen."

By His Stripes (Isaiah 53:5)
"Lord, thank you that you were wounded for my transgressions. You were crushed for my sins. You bore my punishment so that I can have peace and by your stripes we received our healing. In Jesus's name, Amen."

Heal me, Rescue Me (Jer. 17:14)
"Heal me, O' Lord, and I will be healed. Rescue me, and I will be rescued. You are the One that I praise. In Jesus's name, Amen."

Restoration and Healing (Jer. 30:17)
"Lord, restore my health and heal my wounds, so that I will not be considered as an outcast among my people. In Jesus's name, Amen."

Prospering in Health (3 John 1:2)
"Father, bless me so that I am able to prosper in good health even as my souls prospers. Cause me to be a fountain of health and be made whole. In Jesus's name, Amen."

Prayers for Peace, Rest, and Against Anxiety

Turn Anxiety to God (1 Pet. 5:7, Phil. 4:6, Rom. 8:28 GW)
"Lord, I will turn all of my anxieties over to YOU because YOU care for me and I will with thanksgiving, during prayer, make my requests known unto you without worrying about anything because YOU will work it all out for my good. In Jesus's name, Amen."

Perfect Peace (Isaiah 26:3)
"Lord, keep us in in perfect peace as long as our minds are stayed on you. Protect us from the enemy that will try to come and infiltrate the camps of our minds, in Jesus's name Amen."

Favor and Peace (Numbers 6:26 GW)
"Lord look upon me with favor and give me peace, in Jesus's name, Amen."

Peace in the High Places (Job 25:2 GW)
"Lord, authority and terror belong to you. You will establish peace in your high places."

Peaceful Rest (Psalms 4:8 GW)
"Lord, thank you for allowing me to fall asleep in peace and to be able to wake up and see a brand new day. I live securely in YOU. You keep me safe through the night. In Jesus's name, Amen."

Psalms 61:1
"Hear my cry, O God; listen to my prayer. From the ends of the earth I call to you. I call as my heart grows faint; lead me to the rock that is higher than I. For you have been my refuge, a strong tower against the foe. I long to dwell in your tent forever and take refuge in the shelter of your wings."

Psalms 62:1-2
"My soul finds rest in YOU alone; my salvation comes from YOU. You alone are my rock and my salvation; he is my fortress, I will never be shaken."

Hebrews 4:9-11
"Let us strive to enter that rest so that no one may fall by the same sort of disobedience."

Matthew 11: 28
"When I get weary and burdened, I can come to YOU and YOU will give me rest. I take your yoke upon me and I learn from YOU, because YOU are gentle and humble in heart, I know that I can find rest for my soul in YOU."

Financial Prayers

Increase me and my children (Psalms 115:14 KJV)
"Lord increase me more and more, me and my children. In Jesus's name, Amen."

We will Lack No Good Thing (Psalms 34:10 NIV)
"The lions may grow weak and hungry, but because I seek YOU Lord, I will lack no good thing, In Jesus's name, Amen."

The Power to Get Wealth (Deut. 8:18)
"Lord, I will always remember YOU, because you are the one who has given me the ability and power to produce wealth and so you have confirmed your covenant which YOU swore to our ancestors, as it is today."

The Blessing of The Lord (Prov. 10:22 NIV)
"Lord, send forth blessings that will bring wealth without painful toil for it, in Jesus's name, Amen."

The Righteous will not be forsaken (Psalms 37:25 KJV)
"Thank you Lord that I will not be forgotten nor my seed will be begging for bread, not even when we are old."

Deuteronomy 28: 11-13
"Lord grant me abundant prosperity, in the fruit of my womb, the young of my livestock, and the crops of my ground—in the land swore to me by ancestors. ^{12} Lord, open up the heavens and the storehouses of your bounty, to send rain on my land in season and to bless all the work of my hands. I will lend to many nations but will borrow from none. ^{13} Lord you will make me the head and not the tail. Help me to pay attention to the commands that YOU have given to me this day and carefully follow them so that I can always be on top, never at the bottom. In Jesus's name, Amen.

Tithe (Mal. 3:10-12 NIV)
"I will bring the whole tithe in to YOUR storehouse, so that there will be meat in YOUR house. I will test you in this to see if you will not open the floodgates of heaven and pour out so many blessings that there will not be enough room for me to receive it. The Lord will prevent the pests from devouring my crops and the vines in my fields will not drop their before it is ripe. The produce of my land will not be destroyed. The vines of my fields will not lose their unripened grapes. Thank you Lord that this is what you are saying to your people."

Healing Prayer
Lord, you are Jehovah Rophe as such; you are the Lord that heals my body from all manner of diseases, pains and dysfunctions. My body is the temple of the Holy Spirit, therefore, it is functioning in the order that God created it to function. Cells are reproducing other healthy, strong, cells. Blood is freely flowing and there's no clogged arteries and clots preventing its flow. Joints are strong and mobile, there's no stiffness, no inflammation, no pain of any kind because God is a healer and has healed us through his stripes. There are no infirmities that

have afflicted me through my bloodline. God has healed me by every stripe that he has bored upon his body. Every link or attachments to the diseases of my ancestors is broken in the name of Jesus. I walk healthy and prosperous even as my soul prospers. Lord, remove anything that's uncleaned from my bloodline. Remove any cancerous cells that are trying to spread and infect other cells. Send cancer into eternal remission to return no more. I command diabetes and heart diseases to leave our bodies and return to the pit of hell. I walk in healing and I invoke healing to manifest in my life in Jesus's name according to the Holy scriptures, that we were already healed by his stripes. (Isaiah 53:5)

Father, thank you for our healing in Jesus's name Amen.

Prayers for Marriage
Lord thank you that our marriage bed is undefiled. Thank you that our spouses are submissive first to YOU and then to us in everything. Thank you that as Jesus loves the church and laid down his life for her, our spouses are laying down their lives for us in Jesus's name. Thank you for peace, passion, love and effective communication in our marriages. Thank you that we do not deal with our spouses in a treacherous manner, and we love them with a gentle and kind love. Thank you that there's no demeaning or belittling words spoken over our spouse and over us, but with our words we build them up and they build us up. Thank you that as husbands and wives we are ONE in Christ Jesus and we keep God as the third cord in our marriages so that we are not easily broken. We take our marriage vows seriously and we are careful to honor them in Jesus's name. Lord, strengthen our marriages give us strength to endure the differences in opinions or personalities. Give us joy for those times of heated and intense disagreement. Help us to not allow the sun to go down on our anger; but to be reconciled quickly and in a loving manner. Let wives be their husbands' delight and let their husbands find pleasure in their own wives. Don't allow for the counsel or influences of adulterous men or women to draw a wedge in our marriages. Sanctify our marriages so

that we remain a kingdom, divine, union in your sight. In Jesus' name we speak blessings over our marriages, Amen.

Children/Family
Lord, help us to train up our children in the admonition of the YOU so that their peace will be great. Help us to be great examples to our children and family member. Help our loved ones to live lives that are pleasing unto you. Help our children to walk upright before you. When they begin to forget your ways---use your staff and rod to bring them into right fellowship with you. Lead and guide our children help them to see a more excellent way. Lead them in the path of righteousness for your namesake. Revoke the legal access of drugs, alcohol, profanity, and other demonic spirits from our children and family members so that they will not live with any type of addiction; nor will they prematurely die due to any overdose or tragic death because of addictions. We rebuke the hand of the enemy over our children and family members who may not have accepted Jesus as their Lord and Savior. Increase the knowledge of who YOU are in them. Open their eyes to see you in full revelations. Open the eyes of their hearts to receive you, untainted, and without perversion of your truth. Open their ear gates so that they hear your voice and obey ONLY your voice and the voice of the enemy or a stranger they will not follow after nor hear. Lord, help us to be effective gates in the lives of our children and loved ones so that through us they get to know YOU. We speak blessings of restoration, salvation, and reconciliation over our children and family in Jesus's name Amen.

Leadership In America
Lord we pray for the leaders of this great nation. We ask you to endow them with the wisdom they need to pass laws, regulations, bills, and amendments that will not further come against our Christian, godly way of life. Bring them a sense of accountability for every immoral law passed. Help them to see where they are in error and in defiance

against your principles and your commandments. Pluck from their governmental position and assignment all who are wicked in their intentions for the U.S. and who are promoting wickedness. Don't allow for their personal goals and agendas to be carried out as laws for the people. Remove a spirit of anti-Americanism, anti-Christ, and anti-democracy out of the white house. Open the eyes of our President, his cabinet, his administration, the Senate, the House, and Congress and allow for them to see the judgment that their wicked and corrupt leadership has invoked upon this nation. Don't allow for their sins to go unpunished for those leaders who signed bills and passed laws that go against a Christ-like way of life. Lord, bring salvation to the White House. Let our leaders repent and turnaround from any wicked belief system that they have put in place. Dismantle the ungodly traditions of men that's being displayed as doctrines. Dismantle the presence of cultic associations in the government in our churches. Revoke the legal rights to the demonic system of Babylon in our nation. Revoke the legal rights of the demonic spirit of perversion in our nation. Revoke the legal rights of the demonic spirit of deception in our nation. The spirit of lies that has been widely promoted from the President, down to every government officials and even some denominations. Dismantle every illuminati or freemason plots for a new world order in the White House. Expose the corruptive leaders in our government. Destroy the altars in the High governmental places. Destroy all altars to diabolic idols. Destroy every statute in the U.S. to celebrate idol gods such as Shiva, Asterah, the Bull, and Satan. Destroy Them! Destroy their plots and plans against religious leaders, Christians, and their families and children. Protect our people from the choices and consequences of bad leaders. Help America return to her former glory. Help America once again be a hub for Christianity and for the advancement of the Kingdom. God bless America, especially those who are considered righteous by YOU, in Jesus' name we speak blessings of peace, unity over our leaders, Amen.

Deliverance Prayer
Lord, deliver us from all evil and appearances of evil. Deliver us from our enemies who seek to destroy our anointing. Lord deliver us from wolves in sheep clothing who are maliciously spreading false prophecies and teachings. Deliver us from familiar and seducing spirits of influence in our lives, spirit of lust, spirit of distraction, spirit of sabotage, spirit of double-mind, spirit of unrest, spirit of perversion, they all will be destroyed, dismantled, and discouraged from their diabolical assignment in Jesus's name. Deliver us from the terror that flies by day or the arrow that flies by night. Deliver us from them who seek to destroy us through defamation, slandering, black mail, over even inflicting pain. Deliver us from dysfunctional relationships with ungodly ties. Deliver us from all ungodly soul ties. Lord, you are the ONLY one what can deliver us from the day of calamity. Shelter us from the storm approaching. Deliver us from Satan's grip; do not allow him to have a foothold in our lives. We thank you for delivering us, in Jesus's name, Amen.

PART FOUR

Reporting on the Enemy

12

REPORTS ON THE ENEMY

SALUTE REPORT

It's a military acronym which stands for **S**ize, **A**ctivity, **L**ocation, **U**nit, **T**ime, and **E**quipment Report. You may be asking yourself, what does this have to do with spiritual warfare? My answer is: plenty. Where many believers, prayer warriors, and intercessors go wrong is because they cannot identify the enemy nor its weapons. When dealing with spiritual warfare from a military perspective we have to include "reporting" as an intricate part of any strategy against the enemy.

What is the enemy using to trying to bring you down?

Each report must be accurate, done in a timely fashion, and complete. Being a watchman on the wall you must know your enemy. Each prophet knew what they were up against and know your assignment.

In military warfare, studying your enemy and reporting his actions and activities to our higher echelons was imminent in the effectiveness of the battle. Our commanders need to know what the enemy is doing and how he is doing it. We did this through a series of reports. The basic report that ALL guards were required to send was acronymic in the letters S.A.L.U.T.E. We will further explore this report and how it can help us to be effective when combating the Enemy of our Soul.

S (Size of the Enemy You have to know what you are up against. How many are involved?
In spiritual warfare, you must always know the size of your enemy. Is it a stronghold? Which demonic spirit is in operation? The root of the demonic spirit? Point blank you must know what you're dealing with. In real war, we always have to know what we are up against. We research and study the enemy. In spiritual warfare, as guards, we research and study Satan. We must know his size to properly prepare for the size of his attack or possible attacks (plural). (We will discuss this further in another chapter)

A (Activity of the Enemy) what is the enemy trying to engage?
We are implore to know "the devices or tactics" of our enemy. Know how he fights. We have to take note on what it is he's doing. Watchmen watch or (guard) through intercession. Being alert and on our post means we take note of what spirit is in operation and how it operates.

> "...the enemy is seeking whom he may devour..."
>
> *John 10:10*

> "...to and fro roaming the earth..."
>
> *Job 1:1-6*

L (Location of the enemy) Where is the happening at?
In wartime as in spiritual warfare, it's important that the guards take note and report where they see the enemy operating and in whom. Once you identify that there is satanic or cultic activity in operation, then the location (or who) is important. No, we do not divulge our revelations and findings to others. We pray over it. We may discuss it

with other intercessors and report it to the leaders as the spirit dictates. The location is needed to pinpoint the right course of action to take. With the man that had been possessed for many years, the people told Jesus his location. For his deliverance it was important to know where the man was. So they told Jesus that this man was always hanging around the catacombs. Knowing the location of your enemy is advantageous to deliverance. You cannot deliver someone of a spirit if A) you do not recognize the demonic spirit in operation and B) you do not know where it's located or what area of the person's life is affected.

Effective spiritual warfare is all in the KNOW. What you KNOW will help you combat what YOU don't KNOW.

U (Unit) How many demons the Devil has with him?

> *Mark 5:9 says, "And he asked him, What is thy name? And he answered, saying, My name is Legion: for we are many"*
>
> *(KJV).*

In the military, we study other countries insignias, emblems, symbols, and call signs to help us further identify who they are and what are their capabilities. Uniforms tell a lot about a soldier, his unit, and his division or higher echelon. For example, the uniform has the person's name, branch of service, in some cases their skill badges that let you know if their expert riflemen, infantry, pathfinders, airborne or air assault qualified. The patches also tells of the soldiers' unit or division. Combat patches are earned when a soldier has been in combat and under whose authority they fought. As watchmen, we were our patches in how we act, pray, and conduct ourselves in different situation. The vernacular or verbiage of an intercessor tells a lot about how much word they know and how they employ the tools given to them by the word to combat the enemy. What I am trying to convey is simple: learn the different symbols and characteristics that identify each demonic spirit in operation. Don't assume; know exactly what's in operation—if your ultimate goal is deliverance; these things you must know.

T (Time or Timing)
Time may not necessarily be physical time but what season are you in? This is important knowing when God has shifted, knowing when the season has changed, and knowing when the midnight hour is over.

Time is an important factor. In wartime, you must know at what time of the day your enemy is the busiest, when he is dormant or docile, when he is moving, etc. It's important to know that certain spirits attack <u>only</u> at night. While others prefer to attack during the morning; some prefer to attack at specific times throughout the day. Knowing how these spirits operate and when they attack is important. Some spirits attack <u>only</u> during praise and worship. Others may attack while the Word is going forth. Many attack before service even begins. In our personal lives, we are attacked often during our prayer and devotional time with God. Knowing or noting the time of these attacks or the activity of these demonic spirits is important if we are to dismantle, destroy, and discourage their assignments. [***"Everything has its own time, and there is a specific time for every activity under the heaven...a time to tear down and a time to build up"*** Ecc. 3:1, 3b]

E (Equipment) what is the enemy using to trying to bring you down?
When we sent our reports to our higher echelons, we also needed to note the equipment (weapons) of the enemy. By noting their equipment, we could better prepare for combat. For instance, if you saw tanks within the enemy's camp, you would know that they are a field artillery element who has weapons that could possibly take out an entire camp. If you saw mostly antennas, radios, or other communication equipment, then you knew that this enemy was a signal (communications) element. Therefore, you could battle them and cut off the enemy's ability to communicate with other elements or call for

back-up. In spiritual warfare this principle still applies. Knowing the tactics of Satan will better help you defeat his influences over a person's life or region when you know what your enemy uses; you will know which weapons to use to defeat him.

The S.A.L.U.T.E. report was such a basic yet essential tool during early wartime. Now, with all the modern technologies the reports are more digital and less complicated to send, but reporting on the enemy's capabilities is still a very important aspect of effective warfare. All guards <u>must</u> report on what they see and know about the enemy. It's important for deliverance. The key goal of spiritual guard duty should always be: Deliverance. We don't wish that anyone remain in bondage.

When reporting whether in the military or in spiritual warfare, the report must be accurate, done in a timely manner and it must be completed. As intercessors we may report to our leaders and in so doing, we need to know **without a shadow of a doubt that what we are reporting isn't just our own precepts and perceptions, but it is indeed what we see through impartation and discernment.** *Romans 8:26GW states: "At the same time the Spirit also helps us in our weakness, because we don't know how to pray for what we need. But the Spirit intercedes along with our groans that cannot be expressed in words."*

This lets me know that we don't depend just on what we know; but on what HE (the Spirit) knows and it is HE who directs us and leads us in prayer.

Other Reports
SITREP: is a military acronym which stands for Situation report. A SITREP is used as advisement to Commanders on the location and situation and even tactics of the enemy. Why is this useful tool? It gives the Commanders a way of better planning their course of actions or plans of execution. The report is collaborated between the guards (intercessors) and the leaders of the guards (Intercessory Team Leaders) and then it is presented to the Pastor. A situation in a church setting may be dealing with a person who is ill, possessed by

a demonic spirit, or can be identified as being a "potential" threat to the overall atmosphere of the church service or church as a hold. For example, if God has imparted through HIS Spirit that an individual is operating as a "witch"; then we report that to the leaders who then come up with a strategy on how to 1) Protect others from being affected by this spirit 2) Deliverance for the "witch" if they desire to be delivered and 3) Expulsion from church grounds in the event this witch doesn't want to repent. (I have seen a Pastor of mines escorted a woman out of our church service who was seemingly operating in witchcraft and this spirit would make the lady act up during service, especially during the altar call.)

SPOTREP: is a military acronym which stands for Spot report. A SPOTREP is used to when an unknown activity has been identity and this threat is going to affect the unit (church or body of Christ) from accomplishing the mission. All data is collected at the guard (intercessor) level before it is sent up as a SITREP to the Officer of the day (Pastor). This information is passed on to higher authority depending of the severity of the situation.

In the next section, we will be dealing in details with the threat that these demons represent by studying and identifying who they are and how they came to be.

13

IDENTIFYING THE THREAT LEVEL

Why do we identify the threat level?

Let's look at the word: Threat.

Threat n. 1. A statement of an intention to inflict pain, injury, damage, or other hostile action on someone in retribution for something done or not done. 2. A person or thing likely to cause damage or danger; the possibility of trouble, danger, or ruin.

Warfare, whether spiritual or physical, requires that we know who or what we are fighting and their capability. Homeland Security has devise an alert system defining each level of threat. It ranges from low to severe. In the spiritual, we too must assess the level of threat being presented by a devil or demonic spirit. We have to be aware that with each ungodly situation; there's a devil behind it. I know it sounds so far-fetched; but think about it from the infamous phrase: "With each new level there's a new devil." And there's a new plan of attack. Let's define some of these spirits and find out what exactly are we fighting.

> *"For we wrestle not against flesh and blood, but against <u>principalities;</u> against <u>powers;</u> against <u>rulers</u> darkness*

> *of this world; against <u>spiritual wickedness in high places</u>"*
>
> Ephesians 6:12 KJV (emphasis mines)

Let's put a face and a definition to these enemies:

Principality- a ruler; a representative—can be either a monarchical feudatory or a sovereign state ruled or reigned by a monarch. (You may be asking yourself why are we fighting against principalities and what does that have to do with Demons) Glad you asked. Demons have ranking. Did you know that at one point there were three top demons that held positions as princes of the top three Angelic hierarchies?

Yes they did. And just like there's a spiritual ranking or hierarchy there's a demonic because let's face it: that's what Satan does he mimics or copies God.

Powers- 4. A supernatural being: the powers of evil. B. The sixth of the nine orders of angels in medieval Angelogy (Christianity).

Rulers of Darkness- Wickedness or evil; absence or deficiency of light.

Spiritual Wickedness in high places- 1. This entails that there was wickedness (evil; ungodly) in the spirit beings that were said to be "Fallen" angels. But it also implies that there's still wickedness in high places. For example, there's wickedness in the White House which is considered by many as a "high place" because the President resides there and he is a very prominent leader of the free world. We have to exercise wisdom when defining this as it is often taken out of context. (Definition is my own)

Other terms used to identify demons includes:

Cohort- 1. A group or company. 2. A companion or associate. 3. One of ten divisions in an Ancient Roman legion numbering from 300 to 600 members. 4. Any group of soldiers or warriors.

Imp-1. A little devil or demon; an evil spirit. 2. A mischievous child 3. An offspring.

Satan- The chief evil spirit; great adversary of humanity; the devil

Lucifer- a proud; rebellious archangel, identified as Satan who fell from heaven. 2. The planet Venus when appearing as the Morning Star.

Root-The source or origin or of someone or something

Stronghold- A well-fortified place; fortress. 2. A place that serves as the center of a group as of militants or persons holding a controversial view point. (mines…via the Holy Spirit) anything or anyone that poses themselves in your life to hold you back from doing anything of greatness or positive

Demons- An evil spirit with destructive power who opposes God. In his healing ministry Jesus cast out demons out of several people (Matt. 12:22-24, Luke 8:27-39) The Layman's Bible Dictionary George W. Knight and Rayburn W. Ray

Strongman- A person who performs remarkable feats of strength, as in a circus, a political leader who controls by force; dictator. The most powerful or influential person in an organization or business by reason of skill in the formulation and execution of plans, work etc.

(mines...via the Holy Spirit...the strongest demonic representation or possession in your house or in people)

Legion- The major unit of the Roman army consisting of 3,000 to 6,000 infantry troops and 100 to 200 Calvary troops. 2. A large military unit trained for combat; an army. 3. A large number; a multitude; often a national organization of former members of the armed forces. (In Mark 5:9 it was the number of demons possessing one man)

Classifications of Demons
The Lantern of Lights Classifications
Lucifer-Pride
Beelzebub-Envy (envious)
Salthanus-Wrath
Abaddon-Gluttony
Mammon-Greed
Belphegor-Sloth
Asmodeus: Lust

These are also among the "7 Deadly Sins" or the abominations that God hates.

Spina's Classifications of Demons
Based on several criteria:

Demons of Fate

- Goblins
- Incubi (demon male form lies with women in order to engage in sexual activity)
- Succubi-(female demon that appears in dreams in a form of a woman in order to seduce men)

Wandering Groups or Armies of Demons

Familiars

- Assist witches and cunning folk in their practice of magic
- They can appear as animals or human figures (Ghosts)

Drudes

- Malevolent nocturnal spirit (an elf; a hag) associated with nightmares also considered witches
- Demons that are born from the union of a demon with a human being
- Liar and mischievous demons that attack the saints
- Demons that try to induce old women to attend witches Sabbaths (a meeting of those who practice witchcraft and other rites)
- The offspring of an "incubus" or "succubus" and a human.

Mastema

- Hostility
- Adversary
- Actual Satan himself

First Hierarchy of Angels

Princes

1. **Seraphim**-The highest ranking of celestial or heavenly beings
2. **Cherubim** – Winged angelic beings and 2nd highest order of the nine order of celestial Hierarchy.

3. **Thrones-** (Col. 1:16) The carriers' hierarchy of the throne of God. They are considered heroes; warriors (Isaiah 33:7)
4. **Orphanim-** *(Wheels of Galgallin)* **Celestial** beings from Daniel 7:9 also equated with Thrones.

So the story goes that Satan (Lucifer) was one of the highest ranking princes of God's Angelic Host; but he was prideful and arrogant and wanted the Glory that only belongs to God. He orchestrated a rebellion in heaven, and was cast out of heaven. He became a "Fallen" angel. With him several others were cast out as well. A third to be exact. However, why does Paul calls them "principalities?" Because they held positions as "princes" within the First Hierarchy of Angels. Now they are considered "prince" of the air because they can't no longer rule as they once did, they need for us to give them access. They do not create their own "portals" or entry ways; we create them for them through yielding to our sinful nature.

Beelzebub- Prince of the Seraphim, ranking just below Lucifer. Beelzebub along with Lucifer and Leviathan were among the first 3 angels to fall. He tempts people with pride.

Leviathan- Prince of the Seraphim who tempts people into giving themselves to heresy.

Asmodeus- Prince of the Seraphim, burning with desire tempts men to wantonness.

Berith- Prince of the Cherubim, he tempts men to commit homicide; to be quarrelsome; contentious; blasphemous.

Astaroth- Prince of the Thrones- tempts men to be lazy or slothful (lukewarm).

Verrine- Also a Prince of the Thrones tempts men with impatience.

Gressil- Third prince of the Thrones- who tempts men with impurities.

14

DISABLING THE STRONG MAN

> *"How can anyone go into a strong man's house and steal his property? First he must tie up the strong man; then he can go through his house and steal his property."*
>
> **Matt. 12:29 GW**

> *"Let me illustrate this further: who is powerful enough to enter the house of a strong man like Satan and plunder his goods? Only someone even stronger—someone who could tie him up and then plunder his house."*
>
> *– Mark 3:27 NLT*

How do we Tie him up? What do we need to know?

We have to know what weapons to employ and on what type of situation. Obviously, here in the passage of scriptures it is saying: that unless you are stronger than Satan, don't think of going into his house and taking what he thinks belongs to him. We gain our strength by knowing two key things:

1. Who we are in Christ – Our identity plays a very significant role.
2. Who we serve (i.e. the triune Godhead)

Just like in the military, there's a ranking or a chain of command that we must follow in the spiritual realm. We just explored in the last chapter, the enemy's ranking and how they came into power, but our spiritual chain of command is greater than his. In the spiritual, we are dealing with a triune God or the Trinity: three persons, same command or authority, sharing different offices:

1. God the Father- He's over everything; the top officer in charge. The General of Generals.
2. God the Son- God made flesh in the person of Jesus Christ.
3. God the Holy Spirit-He's God's spirit or essence in us.

These three are all in the same; but hold different offices depending on their duties, for example Jesus is said to be:

- The Living Word (John 1:1-4)
- God's only begotten son (John 3:16)
- Savior- (John 3:17, Rom. 5:15-21, Phil. 3:20)
- King of Kings (Dan 5:27, Rev. 19:16, I Tim 6:15)
- Redeemer (Isaiah 44:6)
- Lord (Rom. 5:21, Rom. 4:24, I Tim 1:2, Ephe. 3:11)

This is what is said of the Holy Spirit:

- He is a Comforter (John 14:26)
- You receive the Holy Spirit (Acts 19:2)
- He Builds up your faith (Jude 1:20)

And most important we have God the Father, who has multiple, names because he is omnipotent and multifaceted but here is what He is to me:

- Almighty (Gen. 17:1, Gen. 48:3, Gen. 35:11, Gen. 28:3)
- I AM (Ex. 3:14, Isa. 48:12, Joel 2:27, Lev. 11:44, Isa. 41:10

- Father of Jesus Christ (2 Cor. 1:3, I Thes. 1:1, 2 John 1:3, James 3:9, 2 Pet 1:17)
- Alpha and Omega (Rev. 1:8, Rev.22:13, Rev. 1:11)

God has given us the authority over everything that's demonic. (Luke 10:19) *"Behold I give unto you power (authority) to tread on serpents and scorpions, and over all the power of the enemy (Satan): and **nothing** shall by any means hurt you."* To dismantle the strongman, you have to have strength that comes from having a relationship with the triune godhead. You have to employ the weapons given to you by Almighty God; and then you have to know that YOU have power to destroy, dismantle, and discourage demons. Demons' access can be revoke by you. You have been given that power to be able to decide when you've had enough of the demons and disposed them of their legal rights to stay. We tie Satan up by revoking his access. When he doesn't have legal access to us; then he's dismantled. Demons they dwell in the dry places. These are places where there's no flowing of any kind. Water is symbolic of the Holy Spirit, so in order for you to not become a "dry" place; you must be filled with the Holy Spirit. You must exercise your authority over all the power of the enemy. You have to remind yourself and Satan that you have been given authority (power to influence) over all of *his* power. So we can render his plots and tactics null avoid and useless. You just have to believe that there's power in you.

This power must be evident in your prayers. It is important that you recognize the enemy and fight him fiercely with your prayers. Think of your prayers as weapons that shoot arrows or bullets at the enemy. You're trying to disable him. You are trying to destroy him and defeat him. You don't go into war asking your enemy to please leave you alone. You attack him. You combat him. And you're as relentless as he is in trying to ensure that he will NO longer have access to your home, finances, marriage, family members, church family, church leaders, etc. You do possess the power to do this. Do not go into your war room (secret closet) weak and feeble. Go in there ready to meet the enemy head-on and defeat him. You're not there to negotiate with the enemy; you're there to destroy him. That type of mindset mixed with faith and authority will always help you disarm the strongman. You can go into his camp and take back what he has stolen. You can violently defeat him and ensure that he doesn't have reentry into your life.

Many intercessors need to know this. They need to know that they have the authority to bind Satan up and to send his cohorts, imps, demons, and other wicked spirits packing. You want demons to know your name. You want to let the enemy know that you are on your watch and you are trained and qualified in your assigned weapons: prayer, praise and worship.

It is our hope that this book can really be an eye-opener to all the intercessors and prayer warriors.

Our Watchword
Calvary should be every believer's watch word; but especially those who intercede. When our focus is on the miracle of Calvary; we will not grow weary during our watches. We will stand guard because we know that there's something greater that we are protecting: God's anointing. We should always be mindful of what and who is trying to destroy God's anointing and HIS work. In the military, competence is the watchword of every leader. It is what they need to possess and have in order to ensure the accomplishment of the mission and safety of their subordinates. For us that are spiritual guards, our watchword is Calvary because we should desire that others will join us at the wedding feast. We need to remember that Jesus paid it all and all we have to do is pay it forward by witnessing, interceding, and reaching out to the countless lost souls who are being derailed from their God-given assignment by an evil world system.

Every intercessor should have the mind of Christ operating freely in them so that when you go before the throne of Grace to intercede on behalf of people, nations, ministries, or anything else; we are not posting ourselves as stumbling blocks. We don't want to hinder anyone's prayers from being answered. Our hope is in the fulfillment and accurate execution of each prayer target. We don't want to miss; we want to be expert shooters!

We also are admonished to practice discretion when we are handling others' prayer requests. Sometimes we tend to talk about someone's requests with either other intercessors or people in general. When God gives us a mandate or target; it is for us to pray and do so with the most discretion. We need to learn to be discreet and not talk about what has been entrusted to us by our heavenly Father unless it is for us to publish or tell the individual the Word God has given us. In any case, we need to wait on HIS command. Remember we take all commands from the tower!

   Authors:
   Catherine F. Tukes
   Prophetess Kena P. Jones

ABOUT THE AUTHOR

Catherine F. Tukes, is a devoted, dedicated, woman of God, wife, mother of four, and published author. She is also a disabled Army Veteran. Her passion for writing started at the young age of twelve when she would write poems and short stories. Eventually, her passion evolved to writing college essays for college students, free-lance writing for hire, and writing two Christian Fiction Romance novels as well as Christian Non-fiction book. She is an active member at Kingdom Dominion Church in Villa Rica, Georgia. She serves under Pastor J. Calvin Tibbs and Kimberly Tibbs. She's also a member of the Usher Team, Intercessory Team, and Big Days Event team. She is passionate about helping other women, especially those who are in shelters or recovery homes. She's currently undergoing training to become a Certified Ministerial Coach and also a Peer Specialist to assist men and women who have served in the Armed forces become better versions of themselves.

Prophetess Kena Jones is a devoted woman of God, wife, mother, and Army veteran. She has a passion for serving God's people and is currently serving in Italy over the Women's Ministry at the Chapel. She has worked diligently in God's vineyard as a licensed minister, altar call worker, praise dance team member, and in administrative positions. She is passionate about helping hurting women and God has appointed her for this season to teach women how to be avid ministry members. She is an intercessor and love to pray for God's people and for the nations of the world. Her vision is to serve God through serving others. She is actively planning and steering events that will win souls for the Kingdom overseas.

REFERENCE PAGE

Brand, C. O., Draper, C. W., & England, A. W. (Eds.). (2003). *HOLMAN Illustrated Bible Dictionary.* Nashville, Tennessee: Holman Bible Publishers.

Brook, S. (2015, May 26). *ANSWERS TO PRAYERS.* Retrieved from 8 Prayer Watches – Every Shift Has A Different Anointing: on www.answers-to-prayers.com

Classification of Demons. (2016, January 17). Retrieved from https://en.wikipedia.org/wiki/Classification_of_demons

Dictionary.com. (2016). Retrieved from http://dictionary.reference.com/

Knight, G. W., & Ray, R. W. (1998). *Layman's Bible Dictionary.* Uhrichsville, Ohio: Barbour Publishing, Inc.

Strong, J. (1996). *The NEW STRONG'S COMPLETE DICTIONARY of BIBLE WORDS.* Nashville, Tennessee: Thomas Nelson, Inc.

www.ingramcontent.com/pod-product-compliance
Lightning Source LLC
Chambersburg PA
CBHW071717040426
42446CB00011B/2101